CHINESE RHYME-PROSE

*Prepared for the Columbia College Program
of Translations from the Oriental Classics
Wm. Theodore de Bary, Editor*

CHINESE RHYME-PROSE

Poems in the Fu Form from the Han and Six Dynasties Periods

TRANSLATED AND WITH AN INTRODUCTION

BY BURTON WATSON

Columbia University Press

New York and London

1971

Burton Watson, Professor of Chinese at Columbia University, is the author of *Ssu-ma Ch'ien: Grand Historian of China* (1958), *Early Chinese Literature* (1962), and *Chinese Lyricism: Shih Poetry from the Second to the Twelfth Century* (1971), and the translator of *Records of the Grand Historian of China, translated from the* Shih chi *of Ssu-ma Ch'ien*, 2 vols. (1961), *Su T'ung-p'o: Selections from a Sung Dynasty Poet* (1965), *Basic Writings of Mo Tzu, Hsün Tzu, and Han Fei Tzu* (1967), *The Complete Works of Chuang Tzu* (1968), and *Cold Mountain: 100 Poems by the T'ang Poet Han-shan* (reissue, 1970).

UNESCO COLLECTION OF REPRESENTATIVE WORKS
CHINESE SERIES

*This book
has been accepted
in the Chinese series
of the Translations Collection
of the United Nations
Educational, Scientific and Cultural Organization*
(UNESCO)

Portions of this work were prepared under a grant from the Carnegie Corporation of New York and under a contract with the U.S. Office of Education for the production of texts to be used in undergraduate education. The texts so produced have been used in the Columbia College Oriental Humanities program and have subsequently been revised and expanded for publication in the present form. Copyright is claimed only in those portions of the work not submitted in fulfillment of the contract with the U.S. Office of Education. Neither the Carnegie Corporation nor the U.S. Office of Education is the author, owner, publisher, or proprietor of this publication, and neither is to be understood as approving by virtue of its support any of the statements made or views expressed therein.

To the Memory of Arthur Waley

FOREWORD

Chinese Rhyme-Prose by Burton Watson is one of the Translations from the Oriental Classics prepared under the sponsorship of the Committee on Oriental Studies in order to bring to Western readers representative works of the major Asian traditions in thought and literature. Our intention is to provide translations based on scholarly study but written for the general reader, and especially for undergraduates in general education courses, rather than primarily for other specialists.

The early phases of this project were assisted by a grant from the Office of Education, under the National Defense Education Act, to prepare materials for use in undergraduate general education concerning Asia. It is to the credit of the responsible officials that, in pursuing this aim, they consulted with representatives of the academic community, and were prepared to support the type of program recommended to them as truly in our broadest national interest—one which emphasized the humanistic study of Asia and an appreciation of the basic values in other civilizations.

Chinese Rhyme-Prose celebrates a major poetic form, the *fu*, and one of the most distinctive in Chinese literature. As in Watson's earlier volumes *Early Chinese Literature* and *Chinese Lyricism*, he combines graceful translations with concise commentary and a broad introduction which enhances our comprehension and appreciation of this genre. Professor Watson's translations are by now widely admired, and the number of his contributions to the study of Chinese literature is impressive. I am pleased to observe that this is the tenth book he has contributed in as many years to the Columbia College publication program.

Wm. Theodore de Bary

CONTENTS

CHINESE RHYME-PROSE

INTRODUCTION

SSU-MA HSIANG-JU (179–117 B.C.), one of the earliest and greatest writers in the *fu* or rhyme-prose form, left no statement as to what he thought the characteristics of the form ought to be or how it should be employed.[1] It is probable that, like many artistic creators of genius, he allowed his works to find their own form, without undue worry as to whether in doing so he was abiding by or departing from patterns set by previous writers. There would seem to have been few important works in the *fu* form before his appearance on the literary scene—only one in my selection, Chia Yi's "*Fu* on the Owl," is certainly earlier—and in many respects he is its virtual creator. Nearly all the themes of the typical Han *fu*—the great hunts, palaces, and ceremonies of the capital; rivers and mountains; birds, beasts, flowers, and trees; beautiful women and musical instruments; journeys or meditations on the past—can be traced back to some passage in his works. As the reader will observe when he comes to the "Sir Fantasy" *fu*, Ssu-ma Hsiang-ju adorns his works with an almost endless profusion of scenes and objects, any one of which might be borrowed by a later writer and made the subject of a single poem.

The *fu* in its early form generally consists of a combination of prose and rhymed verse (hence the English term "rhyme-prose"), prose serving for the *hsü* or introduction that explains the genesis of the piece, as well as for occasional interludes, verse taking over in the more rhapsodic and emotionally charged passages. The verse

[1] I set aside the remarks attributed to him in *Hsi-ching tsa-chi* 2, since that text is of such doubtful date and provenance.

I

employs a variety of line lengths, from three-character to seven-character or more, arranged usually in blocks of lines of a uniform length that alternate with one another. A strong preference for the four-character and six-character length is apparent, and many poems are made up almost entirely of such lines. The poem often concludes with a summary in verse called a *luan* or reprise. End rhyme is used throughout the verse portions, as well as frequent alliteration, assonance, and other euphonic effects. Rhetorical devices such as parallelism and historical allusion abound, and the diction is rich with onomatopoeias, musical binomes descriptive of moods or actions, and lengthy catalogues of names, often of rare and exotic objects, that are calculated to dazzle the reader and sweep him off his feet. The *fu*, in fact, though it is a purely secular form, owes much to the shaman songs and chants of the folk religion, incantations empowered to call down deities or summon lost or ailing souls, such as are found in the earlier *Ch'u Tz'u* or *Songs of the South*. The works of Ssu-ma Hsiang-ju in particular seem capable of bewitching one with the sheer magic of rhythm and language, and it is not surprising that Emperor Wu, when he had finished reading one of them, announced that he felt as though he were soaring effortlessly over the clouds.[2]

It was this very exuberance and wildness of language that in some quarters occasioned reservations about the value of works in the rhyme-prose form. The historian Ssu-ma Ch'ien, author of a biography of the poet, reports that when Ssu-ma Hsiang-ju's "Sir Fantasy" was presented to Emperor Wu and his court, objections were voiced that it "overstepped the bounds of reality and displayed too little respect for the dictates of reason and good sense."[3] Ssu-ma Ch'ien himself approves the poem on the grounds that it concludes with a plea for greater frugality in government, and accordingly deserves to be regarded as a *feng*—a work of satire or veiled reprimand. But the fervor with which he argues the didactic worth of Ssu-ma Hsiang-ju's poems suggests that there were many who questioned it.

One of the most important critics to express such doubts was

[2] "Biography of Ssu-ma Hsiang-ju," *Records of the Grand Historian of China*, II, 336.

[3] *Ibid.*, p. 321.

the philosopher Yang Hsiung (53 B.C.–A.D. 18). In his youth he wrote ornate works in the *fu* form descriptive of imperial hunts and outings in the manner of Ssu-ma Hsiang-ju, whom he admired and took as his model, laboring so fervently over one of them, we are told, that he brought on a nervous collapse and was ill for a whole year.4 But later, as he reports in his *Fa yen* or "Model Words," section 2, he abandoned the writing of *fu*. He felt, it seems, that the *feng* or element of reprimand, which was held up as the justification for such works, was too often lost in the torrent of verbiage, and that the effect was often quite the opposite, actually lending encouragement to the Han rulers in their costly and luxurious ways.

The word *fu* had many meanings in ancient Chinese. Among other usages, it was employed as one of a group of critical terms in discussions of the *Shih ching* or *Book of Odes*, where it denoted those songs or parts of songs that were primarily descriptive and straightforward in nature, as opposed to those employing metaphor or allegory. The word *fu* also appears in pre-Han texts signifying a poetical "offering," that is, a song or recital, either original or quoted from the *Book of Odes*, presented by the participants in a social gathering or a diplomatic meeting. Han scholars, with their passion for synthesis, understandably sought to pull together all these various meanings of the word. Yang Hsiung, in his attack on poetry in the *fu* form referred to above, contrasts the Han *fu* with the *fu* or descriptive passages of the *Book of Odes*, declaring: "The *fu* written by the poets of the *Book of Odes* are both beautiful and well-ordered; the *fu* of the rhetoricians are beautiful but unlicensed."5 By "unlicensed" (*yin*) he no doubt meant both extravagant in language and of dubious moral and didactic value.

The historian Pan Ku (A.D. 32–92), author of the *Han shu* or *History of the Former Han*, utilized the same play on the different meanings of the word *fu* to defend the rhyme-prose form and to establish its respectability as a later development of the poetry of the *Book of Odes*. In the preface to his "*Fu* on the Two Capitals" (*Wen hsüan* 1), he describes the *fu* as "deriving from the poetry of ancient

4 See the collected fragments of the *Hsin lun* of Huan T'an, *Ch'üan Hou Han wen* 14/6a in Yen K'o-chün, *Ch'üan Shang-ku San-tai Ch'in Han San-kuo Liu-ch'ao wen*.

5 *Fa yen* 2.

times," and his discussion of the form in the *Yi-wen-chih* or "Treatise on Literature" of the *Han shu* elaborates this connection. (See Appendix I.) This passage in the "Treatise on Literature" represents the earliest extant attempt at a history of the *fu* form. In his eagerness to establish the antiquity of the form, however, Pan Ku in effect makes all pre-Han poetry a variety of *fu*, treating not only the *Book of Odes* but also the works of the late Chou statesman Ch'ü Yüan as though they were examples of early rhyme-prose. Thus, while he forcibly links together in one process of development a number of ancient usages of the word *fu*, he completely obscures the actual evolution of the *fu* form in late Chou and early Han times, creating confusions that unfortunately have carried over into many later descriptions of the form.

Why would a historian attempt to pass off on the world such an unhistorical account of the origin of the *fu* form? The answer would seem to be that, as a writer of *fu* himself, Pan Ku hoped in this way to reconcile his literary endeavors with his Confucian conviction that literature should offer instruction and moral uplift. By tracing the beginnings of the *fu* form back to the *Book of Odes*, which had supposedly been edited by Confucius himself, he could argue that the works of men like Ssu-ma Hsiang-ju, lacking as they seemed to be in didactic value, represented no more than late aberrations, departures from the original intention of the form.

If Pan Ku and those who shared his convictions were not, like Yang Hsiung, to give up *fu* writing entirely, they obviously had to find some way to restore the form to what they saw as its earlier high purpose, to instill true instructional worth into their compositions. They began by eliminating the element of fantasy and hyperbole that had been found objectionable even by Ssu-ma Hsiang-ju's contemporaries. Exponents of rationalism, the main intellectual current of the day, they quite naturally frowned on poems on imperial hunts that pictured the emperor and his attendants flying through the air in their chariots, and substituted more realistic themes and manners of treatment in their own works. Their impulse was probably a wise one. For, even if they had wished to, it is unlikely that they could have successfully recreated the old air of fantasy and verbal magic that had permeated the *fu* of Ssu-ma

Hsiang-ju, or the works of Ch'ü Yüan and his followers from which Ssu-ma Hsiang-ju drew his inspiration.

Some of the difficulties these men encountered when they tried to produce edifying works in the rhyme-prose form may be perceived in Pan Ku's already mentioned *Liang-tu fu* or "*Fu* on the Two Capitals." It is cast in the form of a debate between exponents of the two Han capitals, one speaking in praise of Ch'ang-an, the capital of the Former Han, and the period in history which it represents (206 B.C. to A.D. 8), the other in praise of Lo-yang and the Later or Eastern Han, the period of the writer. In the first section, on Ch'ang-an, the poet allows himself to write in the grand manner of Ssu-ma Hsiang-ju, sparing no eloquence in his portrait of the gorgeous palaces and sumptuous ways of the Former Han court, for all this effulgence is to be censured later in the poem. But when he comes to the second section, in praise of his own ruler and time, he is hard put to create a picture that in interest and richness will even match, much less appear superior to, that of the former age. We are meant to condemn Ch'ang-an's sensuality and applaud the sober mores of Lo-yang, but the language of the poem works against such aims. As so often in literature, vice turns out to be more attractive than virtue, and one can hardly help preferring Ch'ang-an to the bleak and austere classicism of Lo-yang, whose inhabitants

> Are ashamed to wear clothes of fine, sheer-woven fabric,
> Who look down on rare and lovely things and do not hold them dear.

The same problems faced Chang Heng (78–139), the leading *fu* writer of the second century A.D., when he imitated Pan Ku's poem in his *Liang-ching fu* or "*Fu* on the Two Metropolises." Borrowing heavily from his predecessor and expanding the descriptions of the two Han capitals to twice their former length, he labored to invest the Loyang section with additional interest so that it would provide a better balance to that on Ch'ang-an. Thus, in contrast to Pan Ku, who focused almost exclusively on the pomp of the court, he introduces a lively description of a ceremony believed vital to the life and well being of the city as a whole:

> Then at year's end comes the Great Exorcism
> To expel and drive out a host of ills.

The Exorcist seizes his halberd,
Male and female shamans brandish stalks,
With ten thousand good girls and boys,
Vermilion-capped, clad in robes of black;
From peachwood bows, arrows of mugwort
Issue in ceaseless volleys;
Showers of flying pebbles pelt like raindrops
Till the toughest demon is certain to be slain.
Torches, flaming, speed like shooting stars,
Chasing the red pestilence beyond the four borders.
Later the celebrants cross the Lake of Heaven,
Pass over floating bridges,
Destroying *li-mei* devils,
Felling the *hsü-k'uang*,
Cutting down the *wei-t'o*,
Braining the *fang-liang*;
They imprison the "plowing father" under Ch'ing-ling waters,
Drown the "woman-witch" in the Sacred Pond;
They slaughter the *k'uei* and *hsü*, the *wang-hsiang*,
Kill the *yeh-chung*, crush the *yu-kuang*.
Because of them the spirits of the eight directions pale and tremble—
How much more so the *chi-yü* elves and the aging *pi-fang*!
And on Mount Tu-shuo each evildoer
Is eyed by Yü-lü,
Shen-shu to assist him;
One at each arm, the victim is bound with rushes;[6]
Sharply they peer into cracks and crannies,
Seizing and arresting every malicious sprite,
Till the houses of the capital are purified and clean,
Not a one left unsanctified. (*Wen hsüan* 3)

Again, in his description of Ch'ang-an, Chang Heng has tried to add variety and a touch of greater realism, deserting the palaces and royal gardens that are the center of earlier *fu* and conducting the reader into the market place to show him

The hundred tribes of merchants and vendors,
Men and women for whom each sale brings a pennyworth's gain,

---

[6] Yü-lü and Shen-shu were brothers who lived on Mount Tu-shuo and punished demons by binding them with rushes and feeding them to the tigers. Pictures of the brothers were often pasted on doorways for protection.

Peddling good merchandise mixed with bad,
Swindling and hoodwinking the country folk;

or the city's self-appointed rhetoricians and doctors of debate

Gabbling on street corners, arguing in alleys,
Ferreting out every good and evil,
Analyzing down to the tiniest hair,
Probing more than skin-deep, drawing ever finer lines.   (*Wen hsüan* 2)

In another work in what, with the reader's indulgence, might
be called the urban *fu* category, the "*Fu* on the Southern Capital,"
Chang Heng demonstrates a similar interest in homey and realistic
detail. This time he moves into the suburbs of Wan in Nan-yang, the
city which is the subject of the poem, to show us a typical Han farm:

From the streams
Tunnels have been bored that lead the rushing current
Flowing into these rice fields,
Where channels and ditches link like arteries,
Dikes and embankments web with one another;
Dawn clouds need not rise up—
The stored waters find their way alone,
And when sluices are opened, they drain away,
So that fields are now flooded, now dry again,
And the winter rice, the summer wheat
Ripens each in its proper season.
In the broad meadows
Are mulberry, lacquer trees, hemp, and ramie,
Beans, wheat, millet, and paniceled millet,
A hundred grains, thick and luxuriant,
Burgeoning, ripening.
In garden plots
Grow smartweed, fragrant grasses, turmeric,
Sugar cane, ginger, garlic,
Shepherd's purse, taro, and melons.   (*Wen hsüan* 4)

Both the devotion to realism and the fondness for cityscapes
evident in these works of Chang Heng reached their logical cul-
mination in the gigantic "*Fu* on the Three Capitals" by Tso Ssu
(fl. A.D. 300). In a lengthy introduction, translated in Appendix I,
the author criticizes not only Ssu-ma Hsiang-ju but Yang Hsiung,

Pan Ku, and Chang Heng as well, for exaggerations or errors of fact in their descriptions of cities. He, on the other hand, he assures us, has carefully researched the geography of the capitals he intends to depict, has investigated their flora and fauna, studied their folkways and mastered their history, so that he will not be guilty of similar inaccuracies. But though his poem may be factually impeccable, and was apparently much admired by his contemporaries, it fails, it seems to me, on structural grounds. Ssu-ma Hsiang-ju in his "Sir Fantasy" describes three great hunts, those of the feudal lords of Ch'i and Ch'u, and that of the Han emperor; but he is careful to make the descriptions of varying length and complexity so that, as the reader moves from one to another, the poem will build to a climax. Tso Ssu, on the other hand, allots approximately equal space to all three capitals, detailing the same aspects of each and in the same order. As a result, his poem plods along without variation in tempo or intensity, devoid of any real core of interest.

The same tendency toward greater realism is seen in treatments of the travel theme in the *fu* form. David Hawkes, in his illuminating article "The Quest of the Goddess" (see bibliography), has identified the *itineraria* or journey, usually of a magical nature, as one of the characteristic themes of the *Ch'u Tz'u* or *Songs of the South* attributed to Ch'ü Yüan and his followers. We have noted how it is carried over in the works of Ssu-ma Hsiang-ju, in which emperors travel through the sky in carriages. In later works in rhyme-prose form, however, the journey becomes no longer a fantastic aerial flight but a sober progress on land. Thus the "Northern Journey" of Pan Piao (A.D. 3–54), the father of Pan Ku, embodies an account of an actual trip made by the writer as he fled north from Ch'ang-an, though it is given an added dimension in time through the skillful use of historical allusions woven about the various stages of the itinerary. The "Eastern Journey" by Pan Piao's daughter Pan Chao—one can see that it was a very literary family—is even more restrained, hardly venturing beyond a strightforward description of the trip interspersed with expressions of uneasiness appropriate to a well-bred lady and rounded off in Confucian pieties.

With increasing realism came a more personal and subjective note, a turning away from the great public themes of palace, hunt, and royal garden to expressions of private moods and concerns. True, works of this type appear to have been written in earlier times as well, treatments of the *tristia* or disillusionment theme, the other important element which, as Hawkes points out, was taken over by the *fu* writers from the *Songs of the South*. Chia Yi's "*Fu* on the Owl," the second poem in my selection, certainly has as its starting point a very personal experience and predicament, though it moves on to the enunciation of general philosophical principles. And other works, attributed to Tung Chung-shu and Ssu-ma Ch'ien though of doubtful authenticity, express the disgruntlement of the authors at the failure of the world to recognize and make use of their matchless talents, surely as subjective and melancholy a theme as one could find in all *fu* literature.

But so long as the showy, court-sponsored works of Ssu-ma Hsiang-ju and Yang Hsiung continued to attract admirers and imitators, these more modest and personal works remained to some extent outside the mainstream of literary development. It was only when authors, because of moral scruples, rejected the writing of poems that might be construed as encouragements to luxury and lavish spending in government, or when they no longer felt capable of creating viable works on the former grandiose scale, that they began to use the *fu* form with increasing frequency for the expression of personal feelings and experiences.

Many of the late- and post-Han works in my selection belong to this latter category. Wang Ts'an's "Climbing the Tower" was written in the region of the upper Yangtze, far from courts and capitals, to voice the sorrows and frustrations of a lonely traveler. Ts'ao Chih's "Goddess of the Lo" at first reading appears to depart from the prevailing current of realism which I have outlined above, describing as it does a vision of Fu-fei, the goddess of the Lo River, as she reveals herself to the poet. But, unlike the descriptions of supernatural beings in earlier works, this one is enclosed in a carefully factual framework, and it is left to the reader to decide whether to view the goddess as an actual being or merely a figment of the poet's overwrought imagination. Hsiang Hsiu's "Recalling Old Times" and P'an Yüeh's "The Idle Life," as their titles suggest, deal with the private lives and reminiscences of their authors.

Sun Ch'o's "Wandering on Mount T'ien-t'ai" follows the pattern of earlier works on the journey theme, but with one important difference: the journey described in the poem, though it embodies elements from the real world, is clearly identified as taking place solely in the imagination of the poet. Like the ancient shamans, whose bodies remained stationary while their spirits roamed through the universe, Sun Ch'o ascends to the top of Mount T'ien-t'ai, and the religious and philosophical heights which it represents, in mind alone. In this respect his work, like Ts'ao Chih's "Goddess," breaks from the tradition of Han rationalism and seems to be returning to the old wizard world of the *Ch'u Tz'u* poets. The difference is that, while the shamans invariably depicted their peregrinations in terms of breathless exhilaration and ecstasy, Sun Ch'o's mountain top turns out to be a region of profound spiritual calm, even annihilation. The frenzied rapture of the old folk religion has in his work given way to the serenity of Buddhism and philosophical Taoism.

Four post-Han works in my selection stand, in contrast to the above, as later representatives of the relatively objective and impersonal type of *fu*. The first is the "*Fu* on the Sea" by Mu Hua. I have included it not because it displays any substantial advance over the descriptive powers of earlier masterpieces by men such as Ssu-ma Hsiang-ju, but because it applies these powers to a wholly new subject, the sea. The novelty of the subject raises the poem above the level of imitation and gives it a fascination all its own. The second, "The Snow" by Hsieh Hui-lien, belongs to a type of work that was probably common in late Han and Six Dynasties times, a poetic fiction set in the past in which the writer presents his verse as though it were the creation of the great *fu* writers of antiquity. The events described in "The Snow" occur at the court of King Hsiao of Liang in the second century B.C., where Ssu-ma Hsiang-ju and other courtiers are regaling their lord with poetic offerings. In structure, therefore, the piece closely resembles the first work in my selection, "The Wind," attributed to Sung Yü, which also deals with a ruler of antiquity and the entertainment provided him by his court poet and may be a similar fiction of later times. In such works we see the *fu* form being returned to what was probably one of its earliest and most important usages, that of providing a pleasant literary pastime for men of taste, a fitting accompaniment to the pleasures of music, wine, and good fellowship.

Far more somber in tone are the third and fourth works, Pao Chao's "*Fu* on the Desolate City" and Chiang Yen's "*Fu* on Partings." The former is a meditation on the evanescence of worldly glory, a perennial theme in Chinese literature, occasioned in this case by the sight of a once great and prosperous city reduced to ruins. The latter, similarly cast in that most favored of all late Six Dynasties modes, the dolorous, is a poetic catalogue of farewells, a description of the types of separation imposed upon various members of society—the lover, the swordsman, the soldier, the official—evoked through a hundred pathetic details of their dress and surroundings, and those of the loved ones they are forced to leave behind.

The last work in my selection, the "*Fu* on a Small Garden" by Yü Hsin, begins by sounding like P'an Yüeh's account of a happy retreat, but ends on a note of poignant despair. In it, the *fu* is once more restored to its earlier role as a vehicle for the expression of deepfelt and highly personal sentiments.

As my remarks above have perhaps suggested, the *fu* form is a difficult one to handle well. The writer must decide whether he wishes to provide his poem with a prose introduction or interludes, and if so, what proportion of prose to verse is most suitable. He may conclude with a reprise, with songs in a different meter, with a combination of these, or with neither. Above all, he may make his poem as short or as long as he wishes. Unlike Chinese lyric forms, which are often strictly prescribed in length, the *fu* is open-ended, and the temptation, as we have seen in treatments of the famous-city theme, is to make one's own poem just a little bit longer than any previous handling of the theme. A writer in the *fu* form must therefore know when to stop, as well as how to shape and balance the structural elements of his poem, if he is to achieve true artistic success.

Writers of the *fu* in Six Dynasties times, perhaps because they found so much freedom irksome, moved more and more in the direction of increased regularity and compactness of form. Lines of verse, which had often been of irregular length in the early *fu*, now fell invariably into fixed length patterns. As tone became a recognized element in Chinese prosody, precise tonal patterns were added to those of rhythm and syntax, until a new form, the *lü-fu* or tonally regulated *fu*, came into being in the T'ang. A reaction against so much nicety of form took place in the Sung, leading to the creation of another type of work, the *wen-fu* or "prose *fu*," which is so free in form and relaxed in diction that it is hardly distinguishable from ordinary prose.

The last poem in my selection dates from the sixth century A.D. As I have indicated above, the *fu* form, though it had probably seen its finest days, continued to evolve and foster works of importance for many centuries to follow. Something of the magnitude of the literature in the form may be suggested by a description of the *Li-tai fu-hui* or "Collected *Fu* from the Centuries," a compilation of all extant *fu* from earliest times to the end of the Ming dynasty (1644). Completed in 1706, it contains around thirty-five hundred complete works, as well as fragments of others lost long ago, arranged in categories according to theme. It begins grandly with a "*Fu* on Heaven and Earth," from which it can patently move only in the direction of anticlimax. A great many of the works included are quite brief— mere sketches of an object or a mood without any formal beginning or end—but whether they are portions of longer works or are intended to be complete as they stand, it is impossible to judge. Because so many *fu* were written by court poets on the occasion of state ceremonies or banquets or were required as part of the civil service examinations (mainly because they were easy to grade on technical grounds), they tend to be laudatory, even sycophantic in tone, and to deal with felicitous occurrences in the life of the reigning dynasty such as the appearance of auspicious omens, or other topics of a congratulatory nature. Less obviously public in nature, though often the product of court outings and entertainments, are the numberless poems on the subject of particular musical instruments or other artifacts, trees, plants, flowers, birds, beasts, fish, and insects, or those which are designed to evoke particular emotions or moods. Most of the titles, as one might expect from a poetic form so often associated with the *haut monde*, breathe an air of refinement and grandeur, but I am pleased to report that the collection also includes a "*Fu* on Rats," a "*Fu* on Shoes," a "*Fu* on *Fu*" (by the celebrated T'ang poet Po Chü-yi), and, my personal favorite among *fu* topics, a "*Fu* on Sword-swallowing and Fire-eating."

It would of course be presumptuous to attempt to assess the value of such a voluminous body of literature on the basis of an acquaintance with a mere fraction of it. I would like, however, to review some of the criticisms that have customarily been leveled at the *fu* form and to suggest a few of the ways in which, it seems to me, it has contributed to the growth and enrichment of Chinese literature as a whole.

One of the charges most frequently made against the *fu*, particularly by modern, sociologically oriented critics, is that it is representative of one class in society only, that of the ruler and his ministers and courtiers. It is true that nearly all the *fu* were written by scholar-officials (in most periods of Chinese history the only men who had the learning needed to handle such a demanding form), and many of them treat themes associated with the life of the court or the glorification of the ruling house. This unquestionably makes for a certain monotony of subject and tone, as the writers themselves long ago recognized. We have seen how Chang Heng attempted to relieve this monotony by introducing scenes from the life of the common people into his cityscapes, and the same desire to broaden the scope and appeal of the *fu* form is apparent in the works of Sung writers such as Su Tung-p'o. The fact that the rhyme-prose pieces are largely the product of a single class or group in society may well make them less varied or interesting than other types of literature. But, unless one is prepared to argue that the works of one social class are by definition inferior to those of another, I hardly think it makes them less valuable as artistic creations.

A second and more cogent criticism is that the *fu* are excessively obscure and pedantic in language. Certainly many of the *fu*, particularly those of Six Dynasties times, abound in historical allusions, but so do other works of the period in prose or in other poetic forms. Many of the descriptive binomes are hard to pin down in meaning, many of the names in the vast catalogues of wildlife are difficult to identify. But one must remember that such vocabulary is often intended more to astound the reader than to convey to him a clear and comprehensible picture of what is going on. Language, in the *fu*, is being employed in a quite different way from that in which it is used, say, in a simple folk song. And, although the diction of the *fu* may seem tryingly difficult on first encounter, one finds as he reads more works in the form that, like any other genres, it has its clichés and stock phrases, and what earlier appeared recondite soon becomes commonplace. Yang Hsiung is supposed to have advised a scholar who wanted to study *fu* writing under him, "If you read a thousand *fu*, you will be good at writing them."[7] On the basis of personal experience I would venture to add, if you read a hundred *fu*, you will be good at reading them.

A third objection often voiced to the literature in the *fu* form is that it is wearisomely imitative and lacking in novelty. I know of no real rebuttal to such a charge. The later *fu* are indeed imitative of earlier works in the form, but so, for that matter, are later works in the *shih* or *tz'u* poetic forms. One can only note that the Chinese have customarily attached little value to novelty for its own sake, and that their literature, isolated from foreign influence during most of the long centuries of its development, had perforce to grow by feeding upon itself. If the English poetic tradition had begun in 1000 B.C. and continued unbroken to the present, as that of China has, one wonders whether it would have been any more successful in avoiding periods of arid imitation.

The works of genuine interest and importance produced in the *fu* form may be rather few—fewer, perhaps, than in other forms such as the *shih*. But the time and energy which poets have put into *fu* writing over the centuries were by no means a total waste, as some critics would have us believe. First of all, it is obvious that the Chinese derived great enjoyment from the rhyme-prose form. Some men wrote *fu* in hopes of attracting favorable notice from the rulers, others because at certain periods the civil service examination required them to. But many did so because they found it a pleasurable pastime, particularly when undertaken lightheartedly in the company

---

[7] *Hsin lun* fragments, *Ch'üan Hou Han wen* 15/5a.

of friends. The Chinese have always had a passion for occasional poetry, and countless convivial banquets and outings in the countryside were no doubt enhanced by bits of commemorative verse in *fu* form composed on the spot by the guests for their mutual amusement, even though most of the writings of this sort may have disappeared centuries ago along with their creators.

A great many of the *fu*, as I have mentioned, are devoted to descriptions of a single species of plant, tree, bird, or beast, or to a particular type of musical instrument or other artifact. They were often composed at social gatherings, when the object to be described was before the eyes of the group in the garden or hall of the host, and the writers presumably scrutinized it with care before attempting to capture it in verse. At the same time, these being cultured gentlemen, they would consider the associations the object might have with history or legend, what had been said about it by writers of the past, or what symbolism might attach to its form or name. The resulting poem, therefore, in most cases combined both a portrait of the actual object, its appearance and movements, and a recital of the historical, literary, and other associations it called to mind. Because the *fu* is not limited in length, the treatment could be as exhaustive and detailed as the author wished.

I need hardly point out what excellent discipline this provided for the training of poets. It forced them to examine objects closely and to note their peculiarities, to ponder what significance they might have for mankind, and to set forth the results in the highly structured form of rhymed verse. The poems which emerged from this process were sometimes of great beauty. Lu Chi's *Wen fu* or "*Fu* on Literature*,*" to take a famous example, is not only a literary masterpiece in itself, but represents one of the earliest and most penetrating statements on Chinese literary theory. Others, being about "objects" of less universal interest, may be more limited in appeal. But whether a *fu* deals with the moon or the pine tree, the dragon or the lowly cricket, it obviously, aside from its intrinsic merits, is capable of serving as an invaluable source of inspiration for later writers who wish to incorporate these objects into their own creations. Because the *fu* writer has already explored the subject at such length, the writer of *shih* or *tz'u* in the centuries following is often able to select just those details and allusions that will evoke the object most succinctly.

The descriptive and narrative techniques developed in the *fu* form had a profound influence upon the growth of the early five-character *shih*, as a comparison of poems in the two forms by men of the second and third centuries A.D. such as Wang Ts'an and Ts'ao Chih will clearly show, assisting it to grow to maturity in a relatively short space of time. Not only are many of the same images and literary devices carried over from one form to the other, but the diction in the two is also often strikingly similar. Here, for example, is a poem in five-character *shih* form written by Wang Ts'an at about the same time as his *fu*, "Climbing the Tower," which is presented on page 52. The reader who compares the two works will see how closely they resemble each other in mood and imagery.

Tribes of Ching—that's not my home;
how can I stay for long among them?
My two-hulled boat climbs the great river;
the sun at evening saddens my heart.
On moutain and ridge, a last ray of light,
slope and embankment in deepening gloom;
foxes and badgers hurry to their lairs,
flying birds go home to the woods they know.
Sharp echoes wake from the roaring torrents,
monkeys peer down from the cliffs and cry.
Strong winds flap my robe and sleeves,
white dew soaks the collar of my cloak.
I can't sleep at night alone
but get up, put on a robe and play the lute;
strings and paulownia wood know how I feel;
for me they make a sorrowful sound.
On a journey that has no end,
dark thoughts are powerful and hard to bear!

Not only did the *fu* influence the content and diction of the *shih*; in a sense, the *shih* became what it did as a result of the existence of the *fu*. Because a verse form of unlimited length whose main characteristics were lush language and exhaustive treatment was already at hand, the *shih* was free to explore the opposite possibilities, concentrating upon brevity of form, simplicity of expression, and greater depth and suggestiveness. Also, because the *fu* had from early times been utilized for celebrations of the dynasty or other themes of a public nature, the *shih* did not have to be employed for such purposes but could be left for the treatment of more intimate and subjective themes. (The traditional *fu*, with its rather high-flown diction, can of course hardly be used for homey subjects without creating a mock-heroic effect, which is the point of works such as the "*Fu* on Shoes.") This poetic division of labor, I might add, worked all to the advantage of the *shih*, which is one reason why the *fu* of T'ang and later times so often lack appeal—most of the real creative energy, as well as the interesting themes and ideas, are in these periods being channeled off into the *shih*.

As a final example of the type of contribution made by the *fu* to Chinese literature, I will quote a passage describing the *ch'in* or horizontal lute, mentioned in the Wang Ts'an poem quoted above. Though I have not included a representative of this type of rhyme-prose in my selection, such works on musical instruments were very popular in early times and provide valuable information to the student of Chinese musicology. In such pieces, it is customary to begin with an evocation of the wild and beautiful mountain forest where the wood or bamboo from which the instrument is fashioned grows. These passages are among the earliest extended descriptions of nature to be found in Chinese poetry, and as such are of great importance in the later development of landscape poetry. This one is from a work entitled *Ch'i-fa* or "Seven Incitements" by Mei Sheng (d. 140 B.C.), a contemporary of Ssu-ma Hsiang-ju. Brief though it is, it embraces all the principal motifs that, in greatly expanded form, were treated in later works on the subject, and stands as a kind of miniature masterpiece of early rhyme-prose style. The text is found in *Wen hsüan* 34.

> The paulownia of Lung-men soars a hundred feet before it puts out branches, its center spiraling up amid a tangle of dark foliage, its roots sprawling outward this way and that. Above it stand the thousand-yard peaks; below, it peers into a hundred-fathom hollow, while swift torrents and lashing waves eddy and tug about it. Its roots are half dead, half alive; in winter it is buffeted by sharp winds,

settling frost, the driven snow; in summer the sharp crack of thunder and lightning assault it. At dawn yellowbirds and pies are found singing there; at dusk the mateless hen, the lost bird roost there for the night. The lonely snow goose at daybreak calls from the top of it; partridges, sadly crying, flutter beneath its boughs.

Then, when autumn lies behind and steps have turned toward winter, the Lutemaker is sent to fell and whittle it, to fashion a lute, with silk of wild cocoons to make its strings. The buckle of the orphan child is worked for inlay; the ear stones of a widow mother of nine serve as studs.[8] The Teacher T'ang is summoned to display his mastery of the instrument, while Po Ya composes a song for it:

Ears of wheat ripening,
The pheasants at morning fly,
Heading for empty valleys,
Forsaking the withered pagoda tree.
Perched on precipitous cliffs,
They look down on the winding stream.

Flying birds, when they hear its sound, fold their wings and cannot depart; savage beasts, hearing it, droop their ears and go no further. Even crawling insects, crickets and ants, gape openjawed at the tone, unable to advance, for these are the saddest notes in all the world.

[8] So that the lute will take on the melancholy tone of the orphan and the widow.

TRANSLATOR'S NOTE

THERE HAVE BEEN TIMES in the history of English poetry when men delighted in the rolling periods, rich and exotic verbiage, and carefully balanced tropes which characterize the rhyme-prose style, though we do not happen to be living in one of them. At the moment our poets seem to prefer a plainer form and diction, and the nearest equivalent to the *fu* style in modern English is perhaps to be found in the art of the sports announcer, who revels in spates of swift and florid language and takes pride in delivering a nearly endless account of wins and losses without ever repeating the same verb. In my translations of the *fu*, it is first of all this quality of lushness and exuberance that I have tried to capture. Where there are alliterations or other euphonic effects in the original, I have tried to suggest them in English; where parallelisms or allusions occur, I have in most cases carried them over. A special problem is posed by the lists of plant, animal, and other wildlife names, particularly in the Ssu-ma Hsiang-ju piece. Many of them cannot be identified at all, others have only unwieldy Latin equivalents that would hardly fit into a line of English verse. My translations in such cases are often intended only as rough approximations, and I must beg the pardon of specialists if in my ignorance I have credited to ancient China species that could not have existed there. In my translations of the verse portions, one line of English in nearly all cases represents one line of the original. Since the prose passages are highly rhythmical, it is not always easy to decide exactly where prose leaves off and verse begins, and too much importance should not be attached to the line of demarcation as it appears in the translation.

The first three poems in my selection appeared earlier in *Records of the Grand Historian* and *Early Chinese Literature* and are reproduced here with minor revisions; the latter work also contains a discussion of the *fu* of Han times, the main points of which have been recapitulated here. All but one of the thirteen poems in my selection are included in the *fu* section of the *Wen hsüan* or Anthology of Literature, a compilation of the early sixth century, and thus represent works held in high esteem by native critics. I have chosen these poems because I think they suggest something of the richness and variety of the early *fu* and seem to go well into English, in addition to the fact that I like them.

In preparing the present volume I have been aided in particular by the following works: Suzuki Torao, *Fushi taiyō* (Outline history of the *fu*), Tokyo, 1936; T'ao Ch'iu-ying, *Han-fu chih shih-ti yen-chiu* (Historical study of the Han *fu*), Shanghai, 1939; and Nakajima Chiaki, *Fu no seiritsu to tenkai* (The formation and development of the *fu* in Chinese literature), Matsuyama, 1963. Additional translations of *fu* and studies in Western languages are listed in the selected bibliography below.

This book is dedicated to the memory of a man who, among numerous achievements, did much to introduce the *fu* to English readers in the early decades of this century through his translations of works by Sung Yü and others. I knew him only through his writings, but I venture to hope he would approve of this attempt to acquaint readers of English with further works in the form.

SUNG YÜ

3D CEN. B.C.

ॐ

THE WIND

The "Fu on the Wind," preserved in chüan 13 *of the* Wen hsüan *or
"Anthology of Literature," is attributed to Sung Yü, a writer of the third
century* B.C. *who served at the court of the state of Ch'u and was a disciple of
the famous poet-statesman Ch'ü Yüan. The style of the poem, however, and
the fact that it is not recorded in earlier works have led many modern
scholars to question its authenticity. I offer it here not because I believe this
necessarily reflects its proper place in the history of the* fu *form, but for
reasons of expediency alone. It represents a type very important in* fu
literature, the yung-wu *or poetic description of a particular object or
phenomenon, in this case the wind. The poem may be intended simply to
delight the reader with its gusty portrait of the two winds of the land of
Ch'u. But, if commentators are to be believed, a more serious purpose underlies
it, the expression of veiled reproaches against a king whose way of life is so
far removed from that of his impoverished subjects that the very winds that
blow upon them are of a different nature.*

ॐ

KING HSIANG of Ch'u was taking his ease in the Palace of the
Orchid Terrace, with his courtiers Sung Yü and Ching Ch'a at-
tending him, when a sudden gust of wind came sweeping in. The
king, opening wide the collar of his robe and facing into it, said,
"How delightful this wind is! And I and the common people may
share it together, may we not?"

But Sung Yü replied, "This wind is for Your Majesty alone.
How could the common people have a share in it?"

"The wind," said the king, "is the breath of heaven and earth.
Into every corner it unfolds and reaches; without choosing between
high or low, exalted or humble, it touches everywhere. What do you
mean when you say that this wind is for me alone?"

Sung Yü replied, "I have heard my teacher say that the twisted
branches of the lemon tree invite the birds to nest, and hollows and
cracks summon the wind. But the breath of the wind differs with the
place which it seeks out."

"Tell me," said the king. "Where does the wind come from?"

Sung Yü answered:

"The wind is born from the land
And springs up in the tips of the green duckweed.
It insinuates itself into the valleys
And rages in the canyon mouth,
Skirts the corners of Mount T'ai
And dances beneath the pines and cedars.
Swiftly it flies, whistling and wailing;
Fiercely it splutters its anger.
It crashes with a voice like thunder,
Whirls and tumbles in confusion,
Shaking rocks, striking trees,
Blasting the tangled forest.
Then, when its force is almost spent,
It wavers and disperses,
Thrusting into crevices and rattling door latches.
Clean and clear,
It scatters and rolls away.
Thus it is that this cool, fresh hero wind,
Leaping and bounding up and down,
Climbs over the high wall
And enters deep into palace halls.
With a puff of breath it shakes the leaves and flowers,
Wanders among the cassia and pepper trees,
Or soars over the swift waters.

It buffets the mallow flower,
Sweeps the angelica, touches the spikenard,
Glides over the sweet lichens and lights on willow shoots,
Rambling over the hills
And their scattered host of fragrant flowers.
After this, it wanders into the courtyard,
Ascends the jade hall in the north,
Clambers over gauze curtains,
Passes through the inner apartments,
And so becomes Your Majesty's wind.
When this wind blows on a man,
At once he feels a chill run through him,
And he sighs at its cool freshness.
Clear and gentle,
It cures sickness, dispels drunkenness,
Sharpens the eyes and ears,
Relaxes the body and brings benefit to men.
This is what is called the hero wind of Your Majesty."

"How well you have described it!" exclaimed the king. "But now may I hear about the wind of the common people?" And Sung Yü replied:

"The wind of the common people
Comes whirling from the lanes and alleys,
Poking in the rubbish, stirring up the dust,
Fretting and worrying its way along.
It creeps into holes and knocks on doors,
Scatters sand, blows ashes about,
Muddles in dirt and tosses up bits of filth.
It sidles through hovel windows
And slips into cottage rooms.
When this wind blows on a man,
At once he feels confused and downcast.
Pounded by heat, smothered in dampness,
His heart grows sick and heavy,
And he falls ill and breaks out in a fever.
Where it brushes his lips, sores appear;

It strikes his eyes with blindness.
He stammers and cries out,
Not knowing if he is dead or alive.
This is what is called the lowly wind of the common people."

CHIA YI
201–169 B.C.

꩜

THE OWL

"The Owl" by Chia Yi is the earliest work in the fu *form whose authorship and date of composition are reasonably certain. The text is recorded in the biography of the poet in* chüan 84 *of the* Shih chi *or* Records of the Historian *of Ssu-ma Ch'ien, compiled around* 100 B.C. *Moreover, the poem itself is dated with a Han designation that is probably equivalent to the early summer of* 174 B.C., *though some scholars would make it* 173. *Ssu-ma Ch'ien describes the circumstances under which the work was composed: "Three years after Chia Yi became grand tutor to the king of Ch'ang-sha a hoot-owl one day flew into his lodge and perched on the corner of his mat. . . . Chia Yi had been disgraced and sent to live in Ch'ang-sha, a damp, low-lying region, and he believed that he did not have long to live. He was filled with horror and grief at the appearance of the bird and, to console himself, composed a poem in the rhyme-prose style." The position of tutor to the king of Ch'ang-sha, in a remote region of the Yangtze, was actually a form of banishment, and this fact, along with the poet's failing health, accounts for the air of gloom that pervades the work. Using the owl as his mouthpiece, Chia Yi preaches himself a fervently Taoist sermon on the equality of life and death, drawing his ideas and images principally from the writings of Chuang Tzu. His poem, far more personal and overtly philosophical than most of the early* fu, *stands somewhat apart from the mainstream of literary development, its tone too somber for the social uses to which the* fu *form was customarily put, its intense conviction inimitable by anyone not afflicted as its author was.*

꩜

In the year *tan-o,*
Fourth month, first month of summer,

The day *kuei-tzu*, when the sun was low in the west,
An owl came to my lodge
And perched on the corner of my mat,
Phlegmatic and fearless.
Secretly wondering the reason
The strange thing had come to roost,
I took out a book to divine it
And the oracle told me its secret:
     "Wild bird enters the hall;
       The master will soon depart."
I asked and importuned the owl,
"Where is it I must go?
Do you bring good luck? Then tell me!
Misfortune? Relate what disaster!
Must I depart so swiftly?
Then speak to me of the hour!"
The owl breathed a sigh,
Raised its head and beat its wings.
Its beak could utter no word,
But let me tell you what it sought to say:
All things alter and change,
Never a moment of ceasing,
Revolving, whirling, and rolling away,
Driven far off and returning again,
Form and breath passing onward,
Like the mutations of a cicada.
Profound, subtle, and illimitable,
Who can finish describing it?
Good luck must be followed by bad,
Bad in turn bow to good.
Sorrow and joy throng the gate,
Weal and woe in the same land.
Wu was powerful and great;
Under Fu-ch'a it sank in defeat.
Yüeh was crushed at K'uai-chi,
But Kou-chien made it an overlord.
Li Ssu, who went forth to greatness, at last

Suffered the five mutilations.
Fu Yüeh was sent into bondage,
Yet Wu Ting made him his aide.[1]
Thus fortune and disaster
Entwine like the strands of a rope.
Fate cannot be told of,
For who shall know its ending?
Water, troubled, runs wild;
The arrow, quick-sped, flies far.
All things, whirling and driving,
Compelling and pushing each other, roll on.
The clouds rise up, the rains come down,
In confusion inextricably joined.
The Great Potter fashions all creatures,
Infinite, boundless, limit unknown.
There is no reckoning Heaven,
Nor divining beforehand the Tao.
The span of life is fated;
Man cannot guess its ending.
Heaven and earth are the furnace,
The workman, the Creator;
His coal is the yin and the yang,
His copper, all things of creation.
Joining, scattering, ebbing and flowing,
Where is there persistence or rule?
A thousand, a myriad mutations,
Lacking an end's beginning.
Suddenly they form a man:
How is this worth taking thought of?
They are transformed again in death:
Should this perplex you?
The witless takes pride in his being,

[1] Wu and Yüeh were rival states in the southeast during Chou times and Fu-ch'a and Kou-chien the rulers who led them to defeat and glory respectively. Li Ssu, prime minister to the First Emperor of the Ch'in, later fell from favor and was executed. Wu Ting was a king of the Yin dynasty who dreamed of a worthy minister and later discovered the man of his dream in an ex-convict laborer, Fu Yüeh.

Scorning others, a lover of self.
The man of wisdom sees vastly
And knows that all things will do.
The covetous run after riches,
The impassioned pursue a fair name;
The proud die struggling for power,
While the people long only to live.
Each drawn and driven onward,
They hurry east and west.
The great man is without bent;
A million changes are as one to him.
The stupid man chained by custom
Suffers like a prisoner bound.
The sage abandons things
And joins himself to the Tao alone,
While the multitudes in delusion
With desire and hate load their hearts.
Limpid and still, the true man
Finds his peace in the Tao alone.
Transcendent, destroying self,
Vast and empty, swift and wild,
He soars on wings of the Tao.
Borne on the flood he sails forth;
He rests on the river islets.
Freeing his body to Fate,
Unpartaking of self,
His life is a floating,
His death a rest.
In stillness like the stillness of deep springs,
Like an unmoored boat drifting aimlessly,
Valuing not the breath of life,
He embraces and drifts with Nothing.
Comprehending Fate and free of sorrow,
The man of virtue heeds no bounds.
Petty matters, weeds and thorns—
What are they to me?

꙳

SIR FANTASY

According to the biography of him in Shih chi 117, *Ssu-ma Hsiang-ju in his youth served at the court of King Hsiao of Liang, a prince of the Han imperial house who gathered about him an illustrious group of poets and rhetoricians which included Mei Sheng, already quoted in the introduction. While there, he wrote a work in the* fu *form entitled* Tzu-hsü *or "Sir Fantasy." The poem later came into the hands of Emperor Wu, who exclaimed, "What a pity that I could not have lived at the same time as the author of this!" Informed that the author was still very much alive, the emperor summoned Ssu-ma Hsiang-ju to the capital and provided him with writing materials so that he might continue his labors. The poet thereupon revised his earlier* fu *to produce the work that follows, sometimes treated as a single poem entitled "Sir Fantasy," sometimes as two poems, the second entitled "Fu on the Shang-lin Park."*

    Like many early fu, *the poem is cast in the form of a debate, the participants three officials with names that emphasize their fictitious nature, each speaking in praise of his master. In the first part of the poem, presumably that composed at an earlier date, Sir Fantasy of the fief of Ch'u and Master No-such of Ch'i describe the hunts and outings of their respective lords. In the second part, Lord Not-real, spokesman for the supreme ruler, the Son of Heaven, overwhelms his companions with a magnificent description of the Shang-lin Park on the outskirts of Ch'ang-an and the imperial hunts and entertainments that take place there. Surprisingly, the work ends with a passage in which the emperor is shown renouncing such pleasures, opening his parks and ponds to the use of the common people, and adopting a policy of frugality in government. Whether this last represents the real message of the poem, as Ssu-ma Ch'ien, who records the work in his biography of Ssu-ma Hsiang-ju, seems to have believed, or is merely a bow to didactic convention, the reader must decide for himself.*

Emperor Wu was among the most vigorous and strong-willed of early Chinese rulers and under him the empire reached new heights of unity, power, and cultural brilliance. The genius of Ssu-ma Hsiang-ju's poem lies in the masterly way it celebrates this brilliance, making of the Shang-lin Park and its teeming denizens a microcosm of the whole far-flung realm of Chinese dominion and, in the end, of the universe itself. Like the shaman poets of the Songs of the South, *he is in command of all creation, conjuring up its diversity for the delight and wonderment of the reader.*

WHEN CH'U DISPATCHED Sir Fantasy as its envoy to the state of Ch'i, the king of Ch'i called out all the knights within his domain and, providing the party with carriages and horsemen, went out with the envoy on a hunt. After the hunt was over, Sir Fantasy was describing the wonders of the event to Master No-such, while Lord Not-real stood by. When the three of them had taken their seats, Master No-such asked, "Did you enjoy the hunt today?" "Very much!" replied Sir Fantasy. "Did you have a large catch?" Master No-such asked, to which Sir Fantasy answered, "No, the catch was rather meager." "If the catch was small, then what did you find so enjoyable?" he pressed. "What I enjoyed was the way the king of Ch'i was endeavoring to impress me with the great number of carriages and horsemen, while for my part I described to him the hunts which we have at Yün-meng in Ch'u." "Would you perhaps tell us about these hunts of Ch'i and Ch'u?" asked Master No-such, to which Sir Fantasy replied:

"Surely!
The king of Ch'i rode forth with a thousand carriages,
Selecting to accompany him ten thousand horsemen,
To hunt on the borders of the sea.
The ranks of men filled the lowlands;
Their nets and snares covered the hills.

They seized the hares and ran down the deer,
Shot the tailed deer with arrows and snared the feet of the unicorns.
They raced along the briny coves,
The new-felled game staining their carriage wheels.
Their arrows found their mark and the catch was plentiful;
The king grew proud and began to boast of his achievements.
He turned in his carriage and said to me,

"'Does the state of Ch'u also have its hunting lands, its wide plains and stretching lowlands, as rich and joyous as these? Can the hunts of the king of Ch'u rival these of mine?'

"I dismounted from my carriage and replied, 'I am only a humble inhabitant of the land of Ch'u. I have served the king ten years or more, and at times have accompanied him on his travels; I have attended him in the hunting parks of the capital of Ch'u and seen in person what they are like; yet I have not seen all by any means, and I can hardly speak of his hunts in the distant lowlands.'

"'Be that as it may,' said the king of Ch'i, 'tell me in general what you have seen and heard!' and I replied, 'Of course, of course.

"'In Ch'u, they say, there are seven lowlands. Of these I have visited only one; the other six I have never seen. The one I have visited is the smallest of them all, called Yün-meng. It is nine hundred li square, and in the center there is a mountain.

"'A mountain which winds and twists upward,
Rearing its lofty crags on high,
Covered with jagged jutting peaks
That blot out the sun and moon
And entangle them in their folds;
Its crest pierces the blue clouds,
Its slopes roll and billow downward,
Reaching to the Yangtze and the rivers around.
Its soil is colored cinnabar and blue, copper and clayey white,
With yellow ochre and white quartz,
Tin and jade, gold and silver,
A mass of hues, glowing and shining,
Sparkling like the scales of a dragon.

Here too are precious stones: carnelians and garnets,
Amethysts, turquoises, and matrices of ore,
Chalcedony, beryl, and basalt for whetstones,
Onyx and figured agate.
To the east stretch fields of gentians and fragrant orchids,
Iris, turmeric, and crow-fans,
Spikenard and sweet flag,
Selinea and angelica,
Sugar cane and ginger.
On the south lie broad plains and wide lowlands,
Rising and falling in gentle slopes,
Secluded hollows and rolling leas,
Hemmed in by the great Yangtze
And bounded by Witch's Mountain.
On the high, dry crests grow
Indigo, broom, and sage,
Basil, sweet fern, and blue artemisia;
In the low, damp places,
Mallows, henbane, cattails, and bulrushes,
Marsh roses and bog rhubarb,
Water lilies, cress and mare's-tail,
Wormwood and swamp cabbage.
All manner of plants are here,
Too numerous to be counted.
To the west, bubbling springs and clear pools
Spread their restless waters,
Lotus and water chestnut blooming on their borders,
Huge rocks and white sand hidden in their depths,
Where live sacred turtles, dragons, and water lizards,
Terrapins and tortoises.
Northward rise dense forests and giant trees—
Medlar, cedar, and camphor,
Cinnamon, prickly ash, and anise tree,
Chinese cork, wild pear, red willow,
Hawthorn, chinaberry, jujube, and chestnut,
Mandarins and citrons, breathing forth their fragrance.
In their branches live apes, gibbons, and langurs,

Phoenixes, peacocks, and pheasants,
Flying lizards and lemurs.
Beneath their shade prowl white tigers and black panthers,
Leopards, lynxes, and jackals.[1]
The king of Ch'u orders his brave warriors
To seize these beasts with their bare hands,
While he mounts behind four piebald horses,
Riding in a carriage of carved jade.
From pliant staffs of whalebone
Stream banners studded with moon-bright pearls.
He grasps his stout lance forged by Kan Chiang.
At his left side hangs the painted bow of the Yellow Emperor;
On his right are strong arrows in a quiver of the Hsia kings.
A companion as wise as Yang-tzu of old stands by his side;
A driver as skilled as Hsien-a holds the reins.
Though the steeds are reined in to an easy pace,
They gain on the wily beasts;
The carriage wheels run down asses,
The steeds kick at onagers,
Spears pierce wild horses, axle points cut down wild mares,
As the hunters behind their powerful steeds shoot at fleeing jackasses.
Swiftly, relentlessly,
Like thunder they move, like the whirlwind they advance,
Streaming like comets, striking like lightning.
No shot leaves their bows in vain
But each must pierce the eye of the game,
Burrow in the breast, strike through the side,
And sever the cords of the heart,
Till the catch becomes a rain of beasts,
Covering the grass and filling the ground.
With this the king of Ch'u slackens his pace and gazes about,
Raising his head with lofty composure;
He looks toward the dark forest,
Observes the fierceness of his brave huntsmen
And the terror of the wild beasts,

[1] Two lines, mentioning rhinoceroses and elephants and repeating the name of one of the beasts above, have been omitted, as they appear to be a later addition.

Then spurs after the exhausted game, striking those that are spent,
Watching the aspect of every creature.
Next come the lovely maidens and fair princesses,
Robed in fine silk cloth
And trailing rich silks and crepes,
Girdled in sheer netting
And draped with scarves like mist,
Beneath which their skirts, gathered in close pleats,
Gently swirl and sway,
Falling in deep and pliant folds,
So long and full
That they must gather up the hems demurely.
With flying beads and dangling pendants,
They bend and sway in their carriages,
Their robes and scarves rustling softly,
Brushing the heads of the orchids below
Or fluttering against the feathered carriage tops,
Tangling in their kingfisher hairpins
Or twining about the jeweled carriage cords.
Lightly and nimbly they come
Like a vision of goddesses.
Together the groups set out to hunt in the fields of marsh orchids;
Scrambling through the thick grasses
And ascending the stout embankments of the river,
They surprise kingfishers
And shoot crow pheasants,
Fix fine cords
To their short arrows
To shoot the white geese
And the wild swans,
Bring down a pair of egrets
Or a black crane.
Tiring of these sports, they embark
To sail upon the clear lake,
And drift over the surface in their pelican-prowed boats.
They lift their cassia oars,
Spread kingfisher curtains,

And raise feathered canopies;
With nets they snare terrapins
And angle for purple mollusks;
They strike golden drums
And sound the wailing flutes,
As the songs of the boatmen
Echo across the water.
The lake insects are startled
By the waves of their wake,
As the bubbling springs gush forth,
A turmoil of water,
And the boulders in the depths grate together
With a dull, reverberating roar
Like the voice of thunder
Resounding a hundred miles.
To signal the huntsmen to rest from their labors,
The sacred drums are sounded
And beacon fires raised;
The carriages draw up in ranks,
The horsemen form in battalions,
And all take their places in proper order,
Range themselves once more in position.
Then the king of Ch'u ascends the Terrace of the Bright Clouds,
Where he rests in perfect repose,
Takes his leisure in perfect ease
And, flavoring his dishes with herbs and spices,
Sits down to feast.
The king of Ch'u is not like Your Highness,
Who counts it a pleasure to race all day,
Never descending from your carriage to rest,
Slashing at game and staining your carriage wheels with blood.
If I may speak from what I have seen,
The hunts of Ch'i cannot match those of Ch'u!'"

    "With this the king of Ch'i fell silent and did not answer me."
    "How can you speak in such error?" exclaimed Master
No-such. "You have not considered a thousand miles too long a

journey, but have been gracious enough to visit our state of Ch'i. On this occasion the king of Ch'i, calling out all the knights within his domain and providing them with a multitude of carriages and horsemen, has set forth to the hunt, hoping that by these efforts he might secure a plentiful catch and bring enjoyment to the guests at his court. How can you call it a mere boastful show? When he inquired whether you have such hunting lands in Ch'u, it was his wish to hear of the stalwart customs of your great kingdom and to listen to your discourses. Now, instead of praising the virtues of the king of Ch'u, you lavish your words on the glories of Yün-meng and describe to us in rich phrases the wanton pleasures and reckless extravagances which take place there. For your sake, I cannot help wishing you had not done this. Even if these entertainments are as you describe them, they hardly reflect to the credit of Ch'u. If they exist, for you to speak of them is only to spread abroad the fame of your ruler's faults; and if your reports are false, then you do but injure the trust we bear you. To expose the evils of one's ruler or to place trustworthiness in jeopardy—neither action can be approved. By speaking as you have, you must certainly invite contempt from the king of Ch'i and cause embarrassment to the state of Ch'u.

"As for Ch'i, it is bounded on the east by the vast ocean,
And on the south by the mountains of Lang-ya.
We may take our pleasure upon Mount Ch'eng
And shoot game on the slopes of Chih-fu;
Sail upon the Gulf of Po-hai
And roam the marsh of Meng-chu.
Northeast of us lies the land of the Su-shen,
And east of this we border the Valley of Boiling Water.
In autumn we hunt in the region of the Green Hills,
Sailing far away over the seas;
Our state could swallow eight or nine of your Yün-mengs
And they would never even tickle its throat.
As for the wonders and marvels you speak of,
The strange creatures of other regions,
The rare beasts and odd birds—
All manner of beings are gathered here in Ch'i

In such abundance within our borders
That I could not finish describing them,
Nor could the ancient sage Emperor Yü give them names
Or his minister Hsieh write them all down.
Yet, since the king of Ch'i is but a vassal of the emperor,
He does not consider it right to speak of the joys of travel
Or describe the magnificence of his parks and gardens.
Moreover, you are here as his guest,
And this is why he declined to reply to your words.
How could you think it was because he had no answer?"

Thereupon Lord Not-real broke into a smile and said, "The spokesman for Ch'u has spoken in error, while the case for Ch'i leaves much to be desired. When the emperor demands that the feudal lords bear their tribute to his court, it is not that he desires the goods and articles they bring, but that his vassals may thereby 'report on the administration of their offices';[2] and when he causes mounds to be raised on the borders of states and their boundaries to be marked off, these are not for the purpose of defense, but so that the feudal lords may not trespass upon each other's lands. Now, although the king of Ch'i has been enfeoffed in the east to serve as a bastion to the imperial house, he is carrying on secret contacts with the Su-shen and jeopardizing his own state by crossing his borders and sailing over the sea to hunt in the Green Hills, actions which are a violation of his duties. Both of you gentlemen, instead of attempting in your discussions to make clear the duties of lord and subject and striving to rectify the behavior of the feudal lords, vainly dispute with each other over the joys of hunting and the size of parks, each attempting to outdo the other in descriptions of lavish expenditures, each striving for supremacy in wanton delights. This is no way to win fame and gain praise, but will only blacken the names of your rulers and bring ruin to yourselves. Moreover, what do the states of Ch'i and Ch'u possess, that they are worth speaking about? You gentlemen perhaps have never laid eyes upon true splendor. Have you not heard of the Shang-lin Park of the Son of Heaven?

[2] A reference to *Mencius* IB, IV, 5.

"To the east of it lies Ts'ang-wu,
To the west the land of Hsi-chi;
On its south runs the Cinnabar River,
On its north, the Purple Deeps.
Within the park spring the Pa and Ch'an rivers,
And through it flow the Ching and Wei,
The Feng, the Hao, the Lao, and the Chüeh,
Twisting and turning their way
Through the reaches of the park;
Eight rivers, coursing onward,
Spreading in different directions, each with its own form.
North, south, east, and west
They race and tumble,
Pouring through the chasms of Pepper Hill,
Skirting the banks of the river islets,
Winding through the cinnamon forests
And across the broad meadows.
In wild confusion they swirl
Along the bases of the tall hills
And through the mouths of the narrow gorges;
Dashed upon boulders, maddened by winding escarpments,
They writhe in anger,
Leaping and curling upward,
Jostling and eddying in great swells
That surge and batter against each other;
Darting and twisting,
Foaming and tossing,
In a thundering chaos;
Arching into hills, billowing like clouds,
They dash to left and right,
Plunging and breaking in waves
That chatter over the shallows;
Crashing against the cliffs, pounding the embankments.
The waters pile up and reel back again,
Skipping across the rises, swooping into the hollows,
Rumbling and murmuring onward;
Deep and powerful,

Fierce and clamorous,
They froth and churn
Like the boiling waters of a caldron,
Casting spray from their crests, until,
After their wild race through the gorges,
Their distant journey from afar,
They subside into silence,
Rolling on in peace to their long destination,
Boundless and without end,
Gliding in soundless and solemn procession,
Shimmering and shining in the sun,
To flow through giant lakes of the east
Or spill into the ponds along their banks.
Here horned dragons and red hornless dragons,
Sturgeon and salamanders,
Carp, bream, gudgeon, and dace,
Cowfish, flounder, and sheatfish
Arch their backs and twitch their tails,
Spread their scales and flap their fins,
Diving among the deep crevices;
The waters are loud with fish and turtles,
A multitude of living things.
Here moon-bright pearls
Gleam on the river slopes,
While quartz, chrysoberyl,
And clear crystal in jumbled heaps
Glitter and sparkle,
Catching and throwing back a hundred colors
Where they lie tumbled on the river bottom.
Wild geese and swans, graylags, bustards,
Cranes and mallards,
Loons and spoonbills,
Teals and gadwalls,
Grebes, night herons, and cormorants
Flock and settle upon the waters,
Drifting lightly over the surface,
Buffeted by the wind,

Bobbing and dipping with the waves,
Sporting among the weedy banks,
Gobbling the reeds and duckweed,
Pecking at water chestnuts and lotuses.
Behind them rise the tall mountains,
Lofty crests lifted to the sky;
Clothed in dense forests of giant trees,
Jagged with peaks and crags;
The steep summits of the Nine Pikes,
The towering heights of the Southern Mountains,
Soar dizzily like a stack of cooking pots,
Precipitous and sheer.
Their sides are furrowed with ravines and valleys,
Narrow-mouthed clefts and open glens,
Through which rivulets dart and wind.
About their base, hills and islands
Raise their tall heads;
Ragged knolls and hillocks
Rise and fall,
Twisting and twining
Like the coiled bodies of reptiles;
While from their folds the mountain streams leap and tumble,
Spilling out upon the level plains.
There they flow a thousand miles along smooth beds,
Their banks lined with dikes
Blanketed with green orchids
And hidden beneath selinea,
Mingled with snakemouth
And magnolias;
Planted with yucca,
Sedge of purple dye,
Bittersweet, gentians, and orchis,
Blue flag and crow-fans,
Ginger and turmeric,
Monkshood, wolfsbane,
Nightshade, basil,
Mint, ramie, and blue artemisia,

Spreading across the wide swamps,
Rambling over the broad plains,
A vast and unbroken mass of flowers,
Nodding before the wind;
Breathing forth their fragrance,
Pungent and sweet,
A hundred perfumes
Wafted abroad
Upon the scented air.
Gazing about the expanse of the park
At the abundance and variety of its creatures,
One's eyes are dizzied and enraptured
By the boundless horizons,
The borderless vistas.
The sun rises from the eastern ponds
And sets among the slopes of the west;
In the southern part of the park,
Where grasses grow in the dead of winter
And the waters leap, unbound by ice,
Live zebras, yaks, tapirs, and black oxen,
Water buffalo, elk, and antelope,
'Red-crowns' and 'round-heads,'
Aurochs, elephants, and rhinoceroses.
In the north, where in the midst of summer
The ground is cracked and blotched with ice
And one may walk the frozen streams or wade the rivulets,
Roam unicorns and boars,
Wild asses and camels,
Onagers and mares,
Swift stallions, donkeys, and mules.
Here the country palaces and imperial retreats
Cover the hills and span the valleys,
Verandahs surrounding their four sides;
With storied chambers and winding porticos,
Painted rafters and jade-studded corbels,
Interlacing paths for the royal palanquin,
And arcaded walks stretching such distances

That their length cannot be traversed in a single day.
Here the peaks have been leveled for mountain halls,
Terraces raised, story upon story,
And chambers built in the deep grottoes.
Peering down into the caves, one cannot spy their end;
Gazing up at the rafters, one seems to see them brush the heavens;
So lofty are the palaces that comets stream through their portals
And rainbows twine about their balustrades.
Green dragons slither from the eastern pavilion;
Elephant-carved carriages prance from the pure hall of the west,
Bringing immortals to dine in the peaceful towers
And bands of fairies to sun themselves beneath the southern eaves.3
Here sweet fountains bubble from clear chambers,
Racing in rivulets through the gardens,
Great stones lining their courses;
Plunging through caves and grottoes,
Past steep and ragged pinnacles,
Horned and pitted as though carved by hand,
Where garnets, green jade,
And coral abound;
Agate and marble,
Dappled and lined;
Rose quartz of variegated hue,
Spotted among the cliffs;
Rock crystal, opals,
And finest jade.
Here grow citrons with their ripe fruit in summer,
Tangerines, bitter oranges and limes,
Loquats, persimmons,
Wild pears, tamarinds,
Jujubes, arbutus,
Cherries and grapes,
Almonds, damsons,

---

3 In much the same way as the European aristocrats delighted in picturing
themselves as rustic shepherds and sherpherdesses, their Chinese counterparts
loved to imagine that they were carefree immortals riding about on dragons and
sipping dew in airy mountain retreats.

Mountain plums and litchis,
Shading the quarters of the palace ladies,
Ranged in the northern gardens,
Stretching over the slopes and hillocks
And down into the flat plains;
Lifting leaves of kingfisher hue,
Their purple stems swaying;
Opening their crimson flowers,
Clusters of vermilion blossoms,
A wilderness of trembling flames
Lighting up the broad meadow.
Here crab apple, chestnut and willow,
Birch, maple, sycamore and boxwood,
Pomegranate, date palm,
Betel nut and palmetto,
Sandalwood, magnolia,
Cedar and cypress
Rise a thousand feet,
Their trunks several arm-lengths around,
Stretching forth flowers and branches,
Rich fruit and luxuriant leaves,
Clustered in dense copses,
Their limbs entwined,
Their foliage a thick curtain
Over stiff and bending trunks,
Their branches sweeping to the ground
Amidst a shower of falling petals.
They tremble and sigh
As they sway with the wind,
Creaking and moaning in the breeze
Like the tinkle of chimes
Or the wail of flageolets.
High and low they grow,
Screening the quarters of the palace ladies;
A mass of sylvan darkness,
Blanketing the mountains and edging the valleys,
Ascending the slopes and dipping into the hollows,

Overspreading the horizon,
Outdistancing the eye.
Here black apes and white she-apes,
Drills, baboons, and flying squirrels,
Lemurs and langurs,
Macaques and gibbons,
Dwell among the trees,
Uttering long wails and doleful cries
As they leap nimbly to and fro,
Sporting among the limbs
And clambering haughtily to the treetops.
Off they chase across bridgeless streams
And spring into the depths of a new grove,
Clutching the low-swinging branches,
Hurtling across the open spaces,
Racing and tumbling pell-mell,
Until they scatter from sight in the distance.
Such are the scenes of the imperial park,
A hundred, a thousand settings
To visit in the pursuit of pleasure;
Palaces, inns, villas, and lodges,
Each with its kitchens and pantries,
Its chambers of beautiful women
And staffs of officials.
Here, in late fall and early winter,
The Son of Heaven stakes his palisades and holds his hunts,
Mounted in a carriage of carved ivory
Drawn by six jade-spangled horses, sleek as dragons.
Rainbow pennants stream before him;
Cloud banners trail in the wind.
In the vanguard ride the hide-covered carriages;
Behind, the carriages of his attendants.
A coachman as clever as Sun Shu grasps the reins;
A warrior as brave as Lord Wei stands beside him.
His attendants fan out on all sides
As they move into the palisade.
They sound the somber drums

And send the hunters to their posts;
They corner the quarry among the rivers
And spy them from the high hills.
Then the carriages and horsemen thunder forth,
Startling the heavens, shaking the earth;
Vanguard and rear dash in different directions,
Scattering after the prey.
On they race in droves,
Rounding the hills, streaming across the lowlands,
Like enveloping clouds or drenching rain.
Leopards and panthers they take alive;
They strike down jackals and wolves.
With their hands they seize the black and tawny bears,
And with their feet they down the wild sheep.
Wearing pheasant-tailed caps
And breeches of white tiger skin
Under patterned tunics,
They sit astride their wild horses;
They clamber up the steep slopes of the Three Pikes
And descend again to the river shoals,
Galloping over the hillsides and the narrow passes,
Through the valleys and across the rivers.
They fell the 'dragon sparrows'
And sport with the *chieh-ch'ih*,
Strike the *hsia-ko* [4]
And with short spears stab the little bears,
Snare the fabulous *yao-niao* horses
And shoot down the great boars.
No arrow strikes the prey
Without piercing a neck or shattering a skull;
No bow is discharged in vain,
But to the sound of each twang some beast must fall.
Then the imperial carriage signals to slacken pace
While the emperor wheels this way and that,
Gazing afar at the progress of the hunting bands,

[4] These appear to be mythical beasts. From this point on Ssu-ma Hsiang-ju's description of the hunt becomes more and more fanciful.

Noting the disposition of their leaders.
At a sign, the Son of Heaven and his men resume their pace,
Swooping off again across the distant plains.
They bear down upon the soaring birds;
Their carriage wheels crush the wily beasts.
Their axles strike the white deer;
Deftly they snatch the fleeting hares;
Swifter than a flash
Of scarlet lightning,
They pursue strange creatures
Beyond the borders of heaven.
To bows like the famous Fan-jo
They fit their white-feathered arrows,
To shoot the fleeing goblin-birds
And strike down the griffins.
For their mark they choose the fattest game
And name their prey before they shoot.
No sooner has an arrow left the string
Then the quarry topples to the ground.
Again the signal is raised and they soar aloft,
Sweeping upward upon the gale,
Rising with the whirlwind,
Borne upon the void,
The companions of gods,
To trample upon the black crane
And scatter the flocks of giant pheasants,
Swoop down upon the peacocks
And the golden roc,
Drive aside the five-colored *yi* bird
And down the phoenixes,
Snatch the storks of heaven
And the birds of darkness,
Until, exhausting the paths of the sky,
They wheel their carriages and return.
Roaming as the spirit moves them,
Descending to earth in a far corner of the north,
Swift and straight is their course

As they hasten home again.
Then the emperor ascends the Stone Gate
And visits the Great Peak Tower,
Stops at the Magpie Turret
And gazes afar from the Dew Cold Observatory,
Descends to the Wild Plum Palace
And takes his ease in the Palace of Righteous Spring;
To the west he hastens to the Hsüan-ch'ü Palace
And poles in a pelican boat over Ox Head Lake.
He climbs the Dragon Terrace
And rests in the Tower of the Lithe Willows,
Weighing the effort and skill of his attendants
And calculating the catch made by his huntsmen.
He examines the beasts struck down by the carriages,
Those trampled beneath the feet of the horsemen
And trod upon by the beaters;
Those which, from sheer exhaustion
Or the pangs of overwhelming terror,
Fell dead without a single wound,
Where they lie, heaped in confusion,
Tumbled in the gullies and filling the hollows,
Covering the plains and strewn about the swamps.
Then, wearied of the chase,
He orders wine brought forth on the Terrace of Azure Heaven
And music for the still and spacious halls.
His courtiers, sounding the massive bells
That swing from the giant bell rack,
Raising the pennants of kingfisher feathers,
And setting up the drum of sacred lizard skin,
Present for his pleasure the dances of Yao
And the songs of the ancient Emperor Ko;
A thousand voices intone,
Ten thousand join in harmony,
As the mountains and hills rock with echoes
And the valley waters quiver to the sound.
The dances of Pa-yü, of Sung and Ts'ai,
The Yü-che song of Huai-nan,

The airs of Tien and Wen-ch'eng,
One after another in groups they perform,
Sounding in succession the gongs and drums
Whose shrill clash and dull booming
Pierce the heart and startle the ear.
The tunes Ching, Wu, Cheng, and Wei,
The Shao, Huo, Wu, and Hsiang music,
And amorous and carefree ditties
Mingle with the songs of Yen and Ying,
'Onward Ch'u!' and 'The Gripping Wind.'
Then come actors, musicians and trained dwarfs,
And singing girls from the land of Ti-ti,
To delight the ear and eye
And bring mirth to the mind;
On all sides a torrent of gorgeous sounds,
A pageant of enchanting color.
Here are maidens to match
The goddesses Blue Lute and Fu-fei:
Creatures of matchless beauty,
Seductive and fair,
With painted faces and carved hairpins,
Fragile and full of grace,
Lithe and supple,
Of delicate feature and form,
Trailing cloaks of sheerest silk
And long robes that seem as though carved and painted,
Swirling and fluttering about them
Like magic garments;
With them wafts a cloud of scent,
A delicious perfume;
White teeth sparkle
In engaging smiles,
Eyebrows arch delicately,
Eyes cast darting glances,
Until their beauty has seized the soul of the beholder
And his heart in joy hastens to their side.

"But then, when the wine has flowed freely and the merriment is at its height, the Son of Heaven becomes lost in contemplation, like one whose spirit has wandered, and he cries, 'Alas! What is this but a wasteful extravagance? Now that I have found a moment of leisure from the affairs of state, I thought it a shame to cast away the days in idleness and so, in this autumn season, when Heaven itself slays life, I have joined in its slaughter and come to this hunting park to take my ease. And yet I fear that those who follow me in ages to come may grow infatuated with these sports, until they lose themselves in the pursuit of pleasure and forget to return again to their duties. Surely this is no way for one who has inherited the throne to carry on the great task of his forbears and insure the rule of our imperial house!'

"Then he dismisses the revelers, sends away the huntsmen, and instructs his ministers, saying, 'If there are lands here in these suburbs that can be opened for cultivation, let them all be turned into farms in order that my people may receive aid and benefit thereby. Tear down the walls and fill up the moats, that the common folk may come and profit from these hills and lowlands! Stock the lakes with fish and do not prohibit men from taking them! Empty the palaces and towers, and let them no longer be staffed! Open the storehouses and granaries to succor the poor and starving and help those who are in want; pity the widower and widow, protect the orphans and those without families! I would broadcast the name of virtue and lessen punishments and fines; alter the measurements and statutes, change the color of the vestments, reform the calendar and, with all men under heaven, make a new beginning!'

"Then, selecting an auspicious day and fasting in preparation,
He dons his court robes
And mounts the carriage of state,
With its flowery pennants flying
And its jade bells ringing.
He sports now in the Park of the Six Arts,
Races upon the Road of Benevolence and Righteousness,
And scans the Forest of the *Spring and Autumn Annals*.

His archery now is to the stately measures of 'The Fox Head'
And 'The Beast of Virtue';5
His prey is the Dance of the Black Cranes,
Performed with ceremonial shield and battle axe.
Casting the heavenly Cloud Net,6
He snares the songs of the *Book of Odes*,
Sighs over 'The Felling of the Sandalwood'7
And delights in the ruler who 'shares his joy with all.'8
He mends his deportment in the garden of *Rites*
And wanders in the orchard of the *Book of Documents*.
He spreads the teachings of the *Book of Changes*,
Sets free the strange beasts penned in his park,
Ascends the Bright Hall,
And seats himself in the Temple of the Ancestors.

"Then may his ministers freely present before him their proposals for the betterment of the empire, and within the four seas there is no one who does not share in the 'spoils' of this new hunt.9 Then is the empire filled with great joy; all men turn their faces toward the wind of imperial virtue and harken to its sound. As though borne upon a stream, they are tranformed to goodness; with shouts of gladness they set forth upon the Way and journey to righteousness, so that harsh punishments are set aside and no longer used. Finer is this ruler's virtue than that of the Three Sages of antiquity, more plenteous his merits than those of the Five Emperors. When a ruler has achieved such virtue, then may he enjoy himself at the hunt without incurring blame. But to gallop from morn to night

5 Musical compositions supposed to have been played at the archery contests of the king and the feudal lords respectively in ancient times.

6 The name of a constellation.

7 A song from "Airs from the State of Wei," in the *Book of Odes*, said to express censure of a greedy ruler who fails to make use of wise men.

8 From the song "Sang-hu," "Lesser Odes," *Fu-t'ien* section, in the *Book of Odes*.

9 In the passage above the poet uses the hunting metaphor to describe the ideal ruler: a student of the Classics and the arts, amusing himself with the stately dances and songs of antiquity and thinking always of the welfare of his people instead of indulging in extravagant pleasures. Thus, after having dazzled the emperor with his rhetoric, the poet delivers his "message."

in sunshine or rain, exhausting the spirit and tiring the body, wearing out the carriages and horses, draining the energies of the huntsmen and squandering the resources of the treasury; to think only of one's own pleasure before sufficient benefits have been bestowed upon others; to ignore the common people and neglect the government of the nation, merely because one is greedy for a catch of pheasants and hares—this no truly benevolent ruler would do! Thus, from what I can see, the kings of Ch'i and Ch'u merit only pity. Though their domains are no more than a thousand li square, their hunting parks occupy nine tenths of the area, so that the land cannot be cleared and the people have no space to grow food. When one who is no more than a feudal prince attempts to indulge in extravagances fit only for the supreme ruler, then I fear it is the common people who will suffer in the end!"

At these words Sir Fantasy and Master No-such abruptly changed countenance and looked uneasily about, quite at a loss for words. Then, backing off and rising from their places, they replied, "We are uncouth and ignorant men who do not know when to hold our tongues. Fortunately today we have received your instruction, and we shall do our best to abide by it."

CLIMBING THE TOWER

"Ascending to the high places" is cited by Pan Ku (*Appendix I, p. 113*) as one of the occasions upon which fu *are customarily composed. By climbing to a height, the poet expands his horizon and acquires a breadth of vision greater than that which he ordinarily enjoys, in itself an aid to inspiration. With this wider view inevitably come thoughts of his own relative insignifiance, and as his eyes wander in space, so do his thoughts in time. These motifs of the vastness of nature, the relentless passing of time, and the isolation of man are present in the following work by Wang Ts'an, in which the "high place" ascended is a tower, probably situated at the city of Tang-yang on the Chü River, near the place where the Chang River enters it, in present-day Hupeh. To these universal concerns Wang Ts'an has added a very personal note of nostalgia and frustration, for the poem was written when he was sojourning in the region known as Ching or Ch'u, in the upper Yangtze valley, far from his native land. Around* A.D. 195, *the troubled political and social conditions in the north had forced him to flee Ch'ang-an, the Western Capital of the empire, and wander south in search of greater safety. The poem, written some* "twelve years or more" *after this event, expresses the desperate loneliness of the traveler, his homesickness for the north, and his fears that the political situation will never right itself to the point where he may hope to exert his talents in the service of the emperor.*

Intensely lyrical and subjective in tone, in sharp contrast to the preceding work, the poem is entirely in verse, without prose introduction or interlude. The text is preserved in Wen hsüan 11.

Climb the tower so I can see in four directions—
An idle day may help to lessen care.
I scan the ground the building stands on,
Broad and open, few sites to match it,
The lower sweep of the clear Chang angling in on one side,
The other bound by long shoals of the crooked Chü,
Backed by humps and flatlands of the wide plateau,
Looking over marshy borders of the fertile streams,
Reaching north to the range where Lord T'ao lies,
West touching the barrow of King Chao.[1]
Flowers and fruit trees blanket the meadow,
Two kinds of millet rich in the fields,
But lovely as it is, it is not my land—
How have I the heart to stay for long?
Facing troubled times, I set off to wander;
Twelve years and more have slipped by since then;
Thoughts forever taken up with memories of home,
Who can endure such longing and pain?
Propped on the railing, I gaze into the distance,
Fronting the north wind, collar open wide.
The plain is far-reaching, and though I strain my eyes,
They are blocked by tall peaks of the mountains of Ching.
The road winds back and forth, endless in its turning;
Rivers are wide and deep where one would ford.
I hate to be so cut off from my native land;
Tears keep coming in streams I am helpless to check.
Confucius long ago in Ch'en
Cried out in sorrow, "Let me return!"[2]
Chung Yi, imprisoned, played the music of Ch'u;
Chuang Hsieh, though honored, sang the songs of Yüeh.[3]

[1] Lord T'ao, better known as Fan Li, and King Chao are figures associated with the history of the state of Ch'u in the late 6th and early 5th cen. B.C.

[2] *Analects* V, 21.

[3] Chung Yi, a native of Ch'u, was taken prisoner to Chin; when given a lute, he played the music of his homeland. Chuang Hsieh, a commoner of Yüeh, acquired wealth and high office in Ch'u, but when he fell ill, he sang the songs of Yüeh.

All shared this feeling, the yearning for home—
Neither success nor failure can change the heart.
And I think how the days and months glide by,
Waiting for the River that never runs clear,[4]
Hoping to see the king's way at last made smooth,
So I may take to the highroad and try my strength;
I fear to be a bitter gourd uselessly dangling,[5]
A well whose waters, though purified, remain undrunk.
Aimlessly I wander, hesitating, halting;
Suddenly the bright sun is on the point of setting.
Winds, sad and sighing, rise up all around;
The sky darkens till all color has gone.
Beasts peer anxiously, searching for the herd;
Birds call back and forth and beat their wings.
Country fields are empty and unpeopled;
Only the traveler pushes on without stop.
My heart, wounded, stirs in sorrow;
Thoughts are gloomy, drowned in despair.
Rung by rung, I climb down the ladder,
At each step a greater grief cramped in my breast.
Midnight comes and still I cannot sleep;
Brooding, restless, I toss from side to side.

[4] It is said that when the waters of the Yellow River run clear, a sage will appear in the world.

[5] *Analects* XVII, 7: "The Master said, . . . 'Am I a bitter gourd? How can I bear to be hung up and not eaten?'"

TS'AO CHIH
192–232

THE GODDESS OF THE LO

Though the introduction to Ts'ao Chih's fu *on "The Goddess of the Lo"* (Wen hsüan 19), *gives the third year of the Huang-ch'u era as the date of the events that inspired the poem, it is likely that this is a mistake for the fourth year of the era,* A.D. 223, *when the poet had been in the capital, Lo-yang, to pay his respects to his elder brother Ts'ao P'ei, ruler of the Wei dynasty, and was on his way back to his fief in Yung-ch'iu in the east. After a brief description of his departure from the capital, much like that found in one of his poems in the* shih *form dating from the same year,[1] Ts'ao Chih introduces the subject of the work, a beautiful woman who miraculously appears to him on the banks of the Lo River. Since his coachman lacks the power to see her, the poet obliges both him and the reader by presenting an elaborate depiction of her charms. Some critics, not content to accept the vision of the goddess on its own terms, have attempted to impose an allegorical interpretation on the poem, seeing it as a declaration of loyalty addressed by the poet to his brother the emperor; others find the goddess so compelling that they believe her to be modeled after an actual love of the poet's youth.*

IN THE THIRD YEAR of the Huang-ch'u era, I attended court at the capital and then crossed the Lo River to begin my journey home. Men in olden times used to say that the goddess of the river is named

[1] Translated in my *Chinese Lyricism*, pp. 41–43.

55

Fu-fei. Inspired by the example of Sung Yü, who described a goddess
to the king of Ch'u,[2] I eventually composed a *fu* which read:

Leaving the capital
To return to my fief in the east,
Yi Barrier at my back,
Up over Huan-yüan,
Passing through T'ung Valley,
Crossing Mount Ching;
The sun had already dipped in the west,
The carriage unsteady, the horses fatigued,
And so I halted my rig in the spikenard marshes,
Grazed my team of four at Lichen Fields,
Idling a while by Willow Wood,
Letting my eyes wander over the Lo.
Then my mood seemed to change, my spirit grew restless;
Suddenly my thoughts had scattered.
I looked down, hardly noticing what was there,
Looked up to see a different sight,
To spy a lovely lady by the slopes of the riverbank.

I took hold of the coachman's arm and asked, "Can you see her?
Who could she be—a woman so beautiful!"

The coachman replied, "I have heard of the goddess of the
River Lo, whose name is Fu-fei. What you see, my prince—is it not
she? But what does she look like? I beg you to tell me!"

And I answered:

Her body soars lightly like a startled swan,
Gracefully, like a dragon in flight,
In splendor brighter than the autumn chrysanthemum,
In bloom more flourishing than the pine in spring;
Dim as the moon mantled in filmy clouds,
Restless as snow whirled by the driving wind.
Gaze far off from a distance:

[2] A reference to the "Goddess *Fu*" by Sung Yü, in which the poet describes
to King Hsiang of Ch'u a woman of supernatural beauty who visited him in a
dream; the work was apparently one of the principal models for Ts'ao Chih's
poem.

She sparkles like the sun rising from morning mists;
Press closer to examine:
She flames like the lotus flower topping the green wave.
In her a balance is struck between plump and frail,
A measured accord between diminutive and tall,
With shoulders shaped as if by carving,
Waist narrow as though bound with white cords;
At her slim throat and curving neck
The pale flesh lies open to view,
No scented ointments overlaying it,
No coat of leaden powder applied.
Cloud-bank coiffure rising steeply,
Long eyebrows delicately arched,
Red lips that shed their light abroad,
White teeth gleaming within,
Bright eyes skilled at glances,
A dimple to round off the base of the cheek—
Her rare form wonderfully enchanting,
Her manner quiet, her pose demure.
Gentle-hearted, broad of mind,
She entrances with every word she speaks;
Her robes are of a strangeness seldom seen,
Her face and figure live up to her paintings.
Wrapped in the soft rustle of silken garments,
She decks herself with flowery earrings of jasper and jade,
Gold and kingfisher hairpins adorning her head,
Strings of bright pearls to make her body shine.
She treads in figured slippers fashioned for distant wandering,
Airy trains of mistlike gauze in tow,
Dimmed by the odorous haze of unseen orchids,
Pacing uncertainly beside the corner of the hill.
Then suddenly she puts on a freer air,
Ready for rambling, for pleasant diversion.
To the left planting her colored pennants,
To the right spreading the shade of cassia flags,
She dips pale wrists into the holy river's brink,
Plucks dark iris from the rippling shallows.

My fancy is charmed by her modest beauty,
But my heart, uneasy, stirs with distress:
Without a skilled go-between to join us in bliss,
I must trust these little waves to bear my message.
Desiring that my sincerity first of all be known,
I undo a girdle-jade to offer as pledge.
Ah, the pure trust of that lovely lady,
Trained in ritual, acquainted with the Odes;[3]
She holds up a garnet stone to match my gift,
Pointing down into the depths to show where we should meet.
Clinging to a lover's passionate faith,
Yet I fear that this spirit may deceive me;
Warned by tales of how Chiao-fu was abandoned,[4]
I pause, uncertain and despairing;
Then, stilling such thoughts, I turn a gentler face toward her,
Signaling that for my part I abide by the rules of ritual.
The spirit of the Lo, moved by my action,
Paces to and fro uncertainly,
The holy light deserting her, then reappearing,
Now darkening, now shining again;
She lifts her light body in the posture of a crane,
As though about to fly but not yet taking wing.
She walks the heady perfume of pepper-scented roads,
Strides through clumps of spikenard, scattering their fragrance,
Wailing distractedly, a sign of endless longing,
Her voice, sharp with sorrow, growing more prolonged.
Then a swarm of milling spirits appears,
Calling companions, whistling to their mates,
Some sporting in the clear current,
Some hovering over sacred isles,
Some searching for bright pearls,

---

3 The *Book of Odes*, where many exchanges of pledges between lovers are described.

4 Cheng Chiao-fu met two women beside the Yangtze and, unaware that they were goddesses of the river, asked them for their girdle stones. They obliged, but shortly after he had put the stones into the breast of his robe, both the stones and the women vanished.

Some collecting kingfisher plumes.
The goddess attends the two queens of Hsiang in the south,
Joins hands with Wandering Girl from the banks of the Han,
Sighs that the Gourd Star has no spouse,
Laments that the Herdboy must live alone.⁵
Lifting the rare fabric of her thin jacket,
She makes a shield of her long sleeve, pausing in hesitation,
Body nimbler than a winging duck,
Swift, as befits the spirit she is;
Traversing the waves in tiny steps,
Her gauze slippers seem to stir a dust.
Her movements have no constant pattern,
Now unsteady, now sedate;
Hard to predict are her starts and hesitations,
Now advancing, now turning back.
Her roving glance flashes fire;
A radiant warmth shines from her jade-like face.
Her words, held back, remain unvoiced,
Her breath scented as though with hidden orchids;
Her fair face all loveliness—
She makes me forget my hunger!
Then the god Ping-yi calls in his winds,
The River Lord stills the waves,
While P'ing-i beats a drum,
And Nü-kua offers simple songs.
Speckled fish are sent aloft to clear the way for her carriage,
Jade bells are jangled for accompaniment;
Six dragon-steeds, solemn, pulling neck to neck,
She rides the swift passage of her cloudy chariot.
Whales dance at the hubs on either side,
Water birds flying in front to be her guard.
And when she has gone beyond the northern sandbars,

⁵ The two queens are O-huang and Nü-ying, wives of Emperor Shun, who after his death became goddesses of the Hsiang River in the south. Wandering Girl is identified as the goddess of the Han River. The legend pertaining to the Gourd Star is unknown. The Herdboy, another star, is separated from his love, the Weaving Lady star, by the Milky Way, and they are permitted to meet only one night a year.

When she has crossed the southern ridges,
She bends her white neck,
Clear eyes cast down,
Moves her red lips,
Speaking slowly;
Discussing the great principles that govern friendship,
She complains that men and gods must follow separate ways,
Voices anger that we cannot fulfill the hopes of youth,
Holding up her gauze sleeve to hide her weeping,
Torrents of teardrops drowning her lapels.
She laments that our happy meeting must end forever,
Grieves that, once deparated, we go to different lands.

> "No way to express my unworthy love,
> I give you this bright earring from south of the Yangtze.
> Though I dwell in the Great Shadow down under the waters,
> My heart will forever belong to you, my prince!"

Then suddenly I could not tell where she had gone;
To my sorrow the spirit vanished in darkness, veiling her light.
With this I turned my back on the lowland, climbed the height;
My feet went forward but my soul remained behind.
Thoughts taken up with the memory of her image,
I turned to look back, a heart full of despair.
Hoping that the spirit form might show itself again,
I embarked in a small boat to journey upstream,
Drifting over the long river, forgetting to return,
Wrapped in endless remembrances that made my longing greater.
Night found me fretful, unable to sleep;
Heavy frosts soaked me until the break of day.
I ordered the groom to ready the carriage,
Thinking to return to my eastern road,
But though I seized the reins and lifted up my whip,
I stayed lost in hesitation and could not break away.

❦

RECALLING OLD TIMES

*Hsi K'ang (223–62), the subject of this piece, was a celebrated poet, philos-
opher, and lutist, one of the famous group known in legend as the Seven
Worthies of the Bamboo Grove. His "Fu on the Lute" has been translated
by R. H. van Gulik (see bibliography). He roused the ire of the authorities
by attempting to defend his friend Lü An from false accusations, and both
were executed in A.D. 262. Hsiang Hsiu, himself one of the Seven Worthies,
and a witness to these ugly events, wrote this work in memory of his associates.
He and his friends lived at Shan-yang north of the capital, Lo-yang. Wen
hsüan 16.*

❦

I USED TO BE a near neighbor of Hsi K'ang and Lü An. Both were
men of irrepressible talent. But Hsi K'ang was high-minded and out
of touch with the world, and Lü An, though generous in heart, was
somewhat wild. Eventually both of them got into trouble with the
law. Hsi K'ang had a wide mastery of the various arts, and was
particularly skilled at string and wind instruments. When he was
facing execution, he turned and looked at the shadows cast by the
sun, and then called for a lute and played on it.

My travels took me to the west, but later I passed by the old
houses where we used to live. It was the hour when the sun was
about to sink into the Gulf of Yü, and the cold was harsh and

biting. Someone nearby was playing a flute, the sound of it drifting abroad, tenuous and thin. I thought back to the good times we'd had, the banquets and outings of long ago, and, stirred to sadness by the notes of the flute, I decided to write this *fu*.

Obeying orders, I journeyed to the distant capital,
Turned around at last and came back north,
Setting out by boat to cross the Yellow River,
Going by way of my old home at Shan-yang.
I scanned the lonely reaches of the spreading plain,
Halted my horses to rest by a corner of the city wall,
Walked the roads my two friends had once frequented,
Passed their empty houses on the humble lane.
I intoned the "Drooping Millet" with its tears for Chou,
Sorrowed with the "Ear of Wheat" over ruins of Yin,[1]
Thought of the past and those I longed for,
My heart restless, my steps unsure.
Roof and ridgepole still there, unbending,
But those bodies and spirits—where have they gone?
Long ago, when Li Ssu went to his death,
He sighed for his yellow dog with endless longing.[2]
I grieve that Master Hsi had to leave forever,
Looking at the sun and shadows, playing on a lute,[3]
Entrusting his destiny to a deeper understanding,

[1] "Drooping Millet" and "Ears of Wheat" are two songs attributed to ancient times; according to traditional interpretation, they express sorrow over the vanished glories of the Chou and Yin dynasties respectively. The first is #65 in the *Book of Odes*.

[2] Li Ssu (d. 208 B.C.) rose to become prime minister to the First Emperor of the Ch'in dynasty, but was later ousted by a rival and condemned to death. As he was being led to his execution, he said to his son, "I wish you and I were once again tagging after the yellow dog, out the eastern gate of Shang-ts'ai to chase the wily rabbits—but that's all over now!" (*Shih chi* 87.)

[3] One may take the "sun and shadows" as symbolic merely of the approaching twilight of Hsi K'ang's life. But Donald Holtzman, *La vie et la pensée de Hi K'ang* (Leiden: E. S. Brill, 1957), p. 50, believes that Hsi K'ang looked at his own shadow, which stood as proof of his mortality. According to Taoist belief, those who have attained the status of immortal are so pure in substance that they cast no shadow.

Giving his life's remainder to that moment of time.
When I heard the wailing flute with its troubling sound,
Wonderful notes that break and begin again,
I halted my carriage before going farther,
To take a brush and write what is in my heart.

THE IDLE LIFE

P'an Yüeh's "Fu on the Idle Life" (Wen hsüan 16) *begins with a long prose passage describing the thirty years of the writer's career as a government official, a humorously stop-and-go affair of complex advancements, transfers, and resignations. In his account, he stresses the words "inept" and "ineptness" as the refrain of his tale, returning to them repeatedly in order to make clear why in the end he thought it best to retire from politics and lead the life of country squire and filial son at his estate in the southern outskirts of Lo-yang. The poem itself describes the capital in the distance, its temples, schools, army barracks, and other state buildings overflowing into the suburbs; the poet's estate with its orchards and gardens; and the happy life of the family that lived there. Happiness ended in* A.D. 300 *when P'an Yüeh, accused by a disgruntled rival, was executed on charges of treason. According to the harsh custom of the age, his mother, brothers, and other close kin were all obliged to share his fate.*

WHENEVER I READ the "Biography of Chi An," noting that Ssu-ma An four times advanced to the rank of the nine highest ministers, and that the Good Historian characterizes him as "clever at getting along in the official world," I never fail to lay aside the book with a profound sigh.¹ Aha! I say to myself; if even a clever man had such ups and downs, it's no wonder that an inept one should!

It has always seemed to me that, when a man is born into this world, if he is not fortunate enough to be a perfect and matchless sage or a person of subtle and profound understanding, then he must try to gain what merit and achievement he can in the service of the times. If he does so he may, by relying on loyal conduct and observing good faith, go forward in virtue; and by minding his words and establishing a name for sincerity, he may maintain a livelihood. When I was young I enjoyed, undeservedly perhaps, the praise of my fellow villagers, and with all due respect I heeded the orders of the minister of works and grand commandant. The master whom I served was none other than the high minister Duke Wu of Lu.² I was chosen as a "man of outstanding talent" and was made a "gentleman." Later, in the reign of Emperor Wu, the Ancestor of Generations, I became magistrate of Ho-yang and then of Huai. Next I became a palace secretary and then an officer under the commandant of justice.³ While the present Son of Heaven was in mourning, I was appointed secretary to the grand tutor, but when that official was condemned to punishment, my name was stricken from the roster and I was made a commoner.⁴ Later I was suddenly called back to office and made magistrate of Ch'ang-an. I was transferred to the post of erudit, but before I could accept the appointment one of my parents fell ill and I immediately resigned and left my post. Thus, from the time of my capping at the age of twenty until the age when I have learned to "understand fate" [i.e., fifty], I have changed office eight times. Once I rose a step in rank, twice I resigned, once my name was stricken from the roster, once I failed to accept an appointment, and three times I was transferred!

¹ The biography is found in *Shih chi* 120 (*Records of the Grand Historian*, II, 343–52). The "Good Historian" is Ssu-ma Ch'ien, author of the *Shih chi*.

² Chia Ch'ung (217–82), who held the posts of minister of works and grand commandant, was enfeoffed as duke of Lu, and granted the posthumous name of Wu. P'an Yüeh served on his staff.

³ As his biography in *Chin shu* 55 makes clear, he resigned this last post. This is the first of his two resignations.

⁴ The grand tutor Yang Chün was put to death in A.D. 291.

Though all of this starting and stopping may to some extent be the work of fate, still I cannot help thinking that it was largely the result of my ineptness.

A man of great understanding, Ho Ch'ang-yü, once character-ized me as being one who is "inept at using the many talents he possesses." The "many" part of the statement I would not dare lay claim to, but there is ample proof to support the charge of ineptness. At the present time, when "men of outstanding ability hold office" and "the hundred officials are all fitted for their jobs,"5 an inept person would do best to abandon any thought of winning favor or glory. I am still lucky enough to have my mother with me, though she suffers from the ills of age and infirmity. How could I neglect my duty—the duty to wait by her knee and observe what service may please her—merely to charge busily about in pursuance of some peck-and-bushel office?

And so I have turned my eyes toward that life that knows what is enough, that knows where to stop; my desire is now to be like the drifting clouds. I have built rooms and planted trees where I may wander at will in perfect contentment. I possess ponds sufficient for all the fishing I will ever do, and the revenue from my grain-husking operations takes the place of farmlands. I water the garden and sell vegetables to provide something for our morning and evening meal; I raise sheep and peddle the milk products so I can put away a little extra for summer and winter festivals. Filial above all else, friendly to elder and younger brother—this is the way the inept man may perform his "government service."6 And now I have written this *fu* on the idle life in order to describe my activities in song and give vent to my feelings.

I have strolled in the long groves of the Classics and Canons,
Walked the highroads of the wise men of old,

---

5 The phrases are quoted from the *Book of Documents, Kao-yao mo*; there is some doubt as to how P'an Yüeh and his contemporaries may have interpreted the second one.

6 Reference to *Analects* II, 21: "Someone asked Confucius why he did not take part in government. The Master said, . . . 'To be filial, to be friendly to elder and younger brother, these are qualities exercised in government. This then also constitutes a kind of government service.'"

And though I put on a thick-skinned face,
Within, I blush to think of Ning and Chü.[7]
The Way prevails, yet I do not take office;
It prevails no longer, yet I do not act the fool.
What is this but a lack of wit and wisdom,
A superabundance of ineptness and folly?
    So I have retired
To live the idle life on the banks of the Lo,
In body one with the hermit folk,
My name listed among the lower gentry.
The capital at my back, the Yi before me,
I face the suburbs, putting the market place behind.
The pontoon bridge, far-stretching, takes one straight across the
      river;
The Spirit Tower, lofty, lifts its tall form
Where one may spy out hidden secrets of the heavenly bodies,
Trace the start and finish of human affairs.[8]
To the west lie the barracks of the palace guards,
Black-curtained, pennanted in green;
Cross-bows of the *hsi-tzu* and *chü-shu* style,
Different in their firing, in mechanism alike;
Ballista stones, startling as thunder,
Swift arrows like gadflies in flight,
Leading off as the marchers set out,
Lending glory to our Emperor's might.
To the east, the Bright Hall and the Hall of Learning,[9]

---

[7] *Analects* V, 20: "The Master said, 'When the Way prevailed in the state, Ning Wu acted like a wise man; when the Way did not prevail, he acted like a fool.'" *Ibid.* XV, 6: "The Master said, . . . 'A superior man indeed is Chü Po-yü! When the Way prevails in the state, he takes office; when the Way does not prevail, he knows how to wrap up [his talents] and put them away in the folds of his robe.'"

[8] The "floating" or pontoon bridge spanned the Lo River; the Spirit Tower was the imperial observatory.

[9] The *Ming-t'ang* and *Pi-yung*, semireligious and highly symbolic halls of state situated in the suburbs; in the former the ruler sacrificed to his ancestors, proclaimed the principles of his rule, honored elders and worthy men from among the common people, and performed similar ritual acts of virtue.

Holy and majestic, spacious and still,
Their encircling groves a belt of brightness,
The waters that ring them an orbit of deeps.
There filial remembrance pays careful tribute to the father,
Honors noble forebears as the counterparts of Heaven,
Illustrating obedience through respect for wise ancestral ways,
Showing reverence for old age by cherishing the elders.
    And later,
Winter behind us, strolling into spring,
As the yin bows out and the yang spreads abroad,
The Son of Heaven grows busy with his brushwood fires,
Suburban sacrifice to progenitors, a display of duty,
Performance of Vast Music, the Equalizer of Heaven,
Replete with a thousand chariots, ten thousand riders,
Vestments sober and solemn, one in blackness,
Woodwinds tweet-tweeting, shrilling all around,
Luminous, light-filled,
Rich and resplendent,
The bravest aspect that ritual can wear;
Of the king's institutions, the crowning beauty!
Nearby, the two schools are ranged side by side,[10]
Their dual roofs identical,
The right one welcoming the sons of the state,
The left enrolling boys of promise and good report,
Students earnest and well comported,
Keen disciples of Confucian learning,
Some "ascending the hall,"
Others "entering the room."[11]
But learning has no constant master;
Where the Way resides, there it will be found.
And so distinguished statesmen doff their cords of office,
Famous princes hide their seals;
For instruction is like a wind passing over—
Men bow to it as the grasses nod.

[10] Two institutions of higher learning situated near the Hall of Learning, the Kuo-hsüeh for sons of the nobility, and the Ta-hsüeh for talented commoners.

[11] Stages of advancement in learning; see p. 114, n. 7.

This is why benevolence is called the adornment of the village,
Why Mencius' mother moved three times.[12]
    And so I have made my home here,
Building rooms, scooping out ponds.
Tall willows shine in their surfaces,
Fragrant spiny orange planted for my hedge;
Playful fish leap and lash the water,
Lotus blossoms reach out and unfurl.
Bamboo thickets, dense and shady,
The rarest fruits crowding all around;
Pears from Lord Chang's Great Valley orchard,
Persimmons of Marquis Liang's *wu-pi* strain,
King Wen of Chou's supple-limbed jujubes,
Chu Chung's plums from the region of Fang-ling—
None are lacking in these well-stocked groves.
Peach with its twin cousins, walnut and cherry,
Two shades of crabapple gleaming pink and white,
Pomegranate and grape, exotic wonders,
Rambling, luxuriating by their side;
Prune, apricot, almond, and cherry apple
Adding lush and vivid beauty to the decoration,
Flowers and fruit glowing in such splendor
Words cannot describe them all!
    For vegetables we have
Onions, leeks, garlic, and taro root,
Blue-green shoots of bamboo, purple ginger,
Wild parsley and shepherd's purse, sweet to the taste,
Smartweed and coriander, pungent with perfume,
Myoga ginger that hugs the shade,
Legumes whose leaves turn toward the sun,
Green mallows enfolding the dew,
White scallions with frost on their spines.

---

[12] When Mencius was little, his mother moved to a house near a cemetery, but to her distress she found the little boy playing at being a grave digger. She then moved to a house near the market place, but this time found him playing shopkeeper. Finally she moved near a school, where he soon learned to imitate the ceremonies and acts of politeness that were taught there.

And then,
In brisk autumn, when the heat has dispersed,
In shining spring, when the cold is gone,
When the gentle rains have newly lifted
And the six directions are bright and clear,
Then my mother, mounting a plain board carriage,
Climbing up into a light rig,
Rides far off to view the royal environs,
Or, closer, takes a turn about the house and gardens,
Her body pleasantly fatigued by exercise,
The exertion aiding the effects of the medicine,
So that when her tray is brought, she eats all the better,
And her old ailment in time is cured.
Then we roll out the long mats
And line up the grandchildren;
Where willows spread their shade we halt the carriages,
On hillsides gathering purple fruit,
Over the waters angling for ruddy carp,
Sometimes picnicking in the woods,
Sometimes bathing on the riverbank.
My brothers and I, our heads flecked with gray,
Our children still in infancy,
Wish my mother long life, offer a toast,
On the one hand fearful, on the other full of joy;[13]
And as the cup of congratulation is lifted,
Her gentle face beams with delight.
Floating winecups on the water, we drink merrily,
Strings and woodwinds ranged all about;
Stamping feet, we leap up to dance,
Raising voices in boisterous song.
When life offers such peace and joy,
Who would take thought for anything further?
    So I have retired,
To search within in self-reflection,
For truly my accomplishments are paltry and my talents poor.

[13] *Analects* IV, 21: "The Master said, 'One should always know the age of one's parents. On the one hand it will inspire joy, on the other, fear.'"

I have honored Chou Jen's excellent words;
Would I dare exert my strength and step into the ranks?[14]
I can barely keep this poor body alive,
Much less emulate enlightened men and sages!
So with eyes upon the "many wonders,"[15] other thoughts cut off,
Cherishing my ineptness, I will live carefree to the end.

[14] *Analects* XVI, 1: "Chou Jen had a saying: 'He who can exert his strength steps into the ranks; he who cannot stays behind.'"

[15] Epithet for the Way. (Lao Tzu, *Tao-te-ching* 1.)

MU HUA
ca. A.D. 300

THE SEA

To the ancient Chinese the sea was a place of darkness and mystery. At times they ventured out upon it in search of the magic islands of P'eng-lai, Fang-chang, and Ying-chou, home of immortal spirits, that were said to rise from its surface in the Gulf of Pohai or beyond. But for the most part they seem to have conceived of it mainly as the place to which the hundred rivers run. This poem by Mu Hua is, so far as I am aware, the first major work of Chinese literature to take the sea as its topic, though Mei Sheng in his "Seven Incitements" had touched upon the theme, and the writer characteristically works into his subject by way of the hundred rivers. He begins with a retelling of the ancient flood myth, when the hero Yü, serving under the sage rulers Yao and Shun, opened up the waterways and rescued the world from inundation, guiding the rivers so that they flowed harmlessly into the sea. Mu Hua displays great art in portraying the endless movement, the wonder and terror of the sea's waves and tempests, but he appears less interested in, or informed about, the actual creatures that live in and around the sea, and his description of a whale may leave the reader wondering if he had ever seen one. The lack of a distinct formal preface or concluding section has disturbed some commentators, but I think the reader will agree that the poem functions quite satisfactorily without them. Wen hsüan 12.

Long ago, when Emperor Shun of Kuei was still minister to
      Yao of T'ang,
The Heaven-appointed waterways swelled and overflowed,

72

Causing blight, causing affliction;
Giant billows, fiercely raging,
Swept ten thousand li unbounded,
Long waves that gather and build,
Rolling abroad in eight directions.
    Then it was that Yü
Sliced through the banks and ridges that loom along the waters,
Pierced the ponds and reservoirs to let them drain;
Broke open the cliffs and crags of Lung-men,
Severing hills and ranges, hacking and chiseling through.
And when the crowded mountains had been subdued,
The hundred rivers drawn off in sunken channels,
Then the massed waters in their depth and power
Rose up, toppled, and sped on their way.
When he had guided the Yellow River and the Yangtze,
The myriad sluices so they flowed together,
Then the Five Mountains plucked themselves up,
And the Nine Continents came forth as dry land.
Drops and driblets, the smallest ooze,
Damp congestion of cloud and fog,
The least rivulet that trickles and trills—
There was none that failed to come draining down.
Ah, the vastness of the magic sea,
Eternally receiving and taking them in,
Its breadth and its strangeness
A fitting match for the gigantic size of it!
    This is its form:
A watery wasteland, tossing, heaving,
The sky afloat on it, no coast in sight;
Fathomless, limitless,
Bottomless, unending,
With waves like chains of mountains,
Now linking, now shattering,
Sucking in and spewing back the hundred rivers,
Washing clear the Huai and the Han,
Inundating the broad embankments,
Immense and borderless, trackless and wild.

And when night's bright chariot
Has turned rein toward the caves of Chin-shu,
When the winging fire of day starts up from Fu-sang fords,
And wind-driven sands, rustling and sighing,
Scurry over the beaches of the islands,
Then with a pounding fury
The giant combers lift and sway,
Thumping and jarring one against another,
Flinging foam, tossing up their crests,
In form like wheels of heaven dizzily spinning,
Or axles of the earth sticking up and turning round;
Like jagged peaks that climb the air to fall back again,
Or the Five Mountains drumming and dancing, hammering one
　　　　　　another,
Jostling, stumbling, piling up in heaps,
Suddenly bulging into knolls and declivities,
Whirling, sucking down to form hollows,
Now shooting skyward in lonely pinnacles.
Schools of little waves dart off at an angle,
While hulking giants rear and crash together;
Waves in panic flee with lightning quickness,
Frightened waters huddle close together,
Parting, closing, breaking, joining,
Ceaselessly, restlessly,
Troubled and turbulent,
Hissing with spume.
And when the clouds of dust and darkness have settled and gone,
No longer racing, no longer scudding by,
When the lightest grain of sand no longer stirs,
And the vine's slimmest tendrils dangle unmoved,
Still there is the gape and suck,
The solitary churning of the waves left over,
Sloshing, pitching,
Molding themselves into hummocks and hills
Whose coves in turn are drowned by tides,
Whose waters brim over to cut new beds,
Turning their backs on barbarian lands,

Rolling and tumbling ten thousand li.
    Should it happen that
Sudden news comes from wild and distant regions,
The king's command to be speedily relayed,
Then fleet horses set out, sculling oars are labored,
The former to cross the mountains, the latter to span the sea.
Then we watch for a vigorous wind,
Step the hundred-foot mast,
Rig the lengthy lines,
Hoist the jibs and sails,
Scan the surf, then take our long farewell,
Gliding off, a bird in flight,
Sudden as a wary duck parted from its mate,
Swift, as though drawn by six dragons,
In one bound, three thousand li:
Less than a morning and already we've reached our destination!
But should a man approach the deeps with guilt on his back,
A violator of oaths, a false invocator,
Then the sea elves impede his progress,
Horse monsters stand in his way,
The god T'ien-wu shows his dim semblance,
The demon Wang-hsiang of a sudden appears;
A host of wonders meets and confronts him,
Weird and freakish things he sees.
Tearing the sails, splitting the mast,
Violent winds come to work mischief,
Immense in magic transformations,
Sudden as the pall of evening,
Their breath like the mists of heaven,
Banks of vapor rolling in like clouds.
Streaks of precipitate lightning
Illumine a hundred unearthly colors,
Abruptly flashing, abruptly gone,
Blinding, dazzling the eye without measure.
Rushing waters clash together,
Frenzied forces that collide,
Like clouds that crumble, sheets of rain descending,

Humming, moaning,
Whooshing forward, reeling back,
Bunching and straining apart,
Roaring and reverberating,
Dousing the cloud banks, washing the sun.
Then the sailors and fishermen
Voyage south, explore the edges of the east,
Some to end crushed in caves of loggerhead and sea lizard,
Some caught and impaled on ragged mountain peaks,
Some buffeted and blown to the country of naked men,
Some floating far off to the Black Tooth land,
Some drifting like duckweed, bobbing, circling,
Some, wafted on homing winds, finding their way back,
Knowing only that the wonders they've seen were many and
                fearsome,
Witless whether the route they came by was near or far.
        These are its dimensions:
South it batters the Vermilion Cliffs,
North washes the Waste of Heaven,
East extends as far as Split Tree,
West presses on Ch'ing and Hsü,
Its expanse incalculable,
Tens of thousands of li and more.
It breathes forth clouds and rainbows,
Shelters dragons and fish,
Conceals the scaly K'un,
Hides spirit dwellings.
Is it only T'ai-tien's priceless shell,
The bright pearl of Marquis Sui that it holds in store?
These the world's collectors all have heard of,
But those others—the unnamed ones—they do not know exist.
Marvels rarely heard of in this world—
How should one know their names in full?
So I can only suggest their colors,
Only dimly sketch their forms.
Within those watery treasure houses,
Those courts unfathomably deep,
Are tall islands, borne by the sea turtle,

Reaching skyward, lofty and alone,
Clearing the huge billows,
Pointing toward the great pure air,
Flaunting massive boulders,
Home for a hundred immortal spirits.
When southern winds bluster, the islands march southward;
In the face of northern winds, they travel north.[1]
The sea's confines hold heavenly jewels, water wonders,
The halls of the shark-man,[2]
Flawed gems that sparkle strangely,
Scaled and armored beings of odd design.
Patterns like cloud brocade are flung
Across the face of the sandy shore;
Tints like those of shimmering damask
Play about the lips of whorled shell and clam.
Multitudes of colors parade their brilliance,
Ten thousand hues hold their freshness hidden,
Sun-warmed ice that never melts,
Shadowy fires that burn in secret,
Smoldering charcoal flaring up again,
Casting its glow over the earth's nine springs,
Scarlet flames, green smoke,
Leaping, spiraling upward and away.[3]
For fish there is the sea-straddling whale,
Humped and lordly, swimming alone,
Scraping the mountain's back,
Pillowing on tall billows,
Feeding on scaly and crustaceous creatures,
Gobbling up even dragon-sized boats.
When he sucks in the waves then the tallest surfs come tumbling;
When he blows on the billows then the hundred streams
        flow backward.

[1] Because the monstrous turtle that bears the magic islands on its back always moves in the opposite direction to the wind.

[2] A creature half fish, half man; his tears become pearls.

[3] The passage on ice and smoldering fires may be taken to refer to the iridescent colors of the nacreous shells.

And should he flounder where the waves run thin,
Should he die stranded on salty flats,
His huge scales will pierce the clouds,
His dorsal fins stab the sky;
The bones of his skull will turn into a mountain,
The oils that exude from him collect in deep pools.
Meanwhile, in crevices of cliff and promontory,
By scarps carved of gravel and sand,
Winged and feathered creatures rear their young,
Pecking the eggs to let the chicks out,
Ducklings, a ball of fuzz,
Baby storks, their down still wet.
Winging in flocks, diving side by side,
They play about the open places, float on the deeps,
Tagging and tailing after one another,
Dipping and soaring;
Their restless fluttering raises a thunder,
Their milling flights become a forest,
Screeching and shrilling back and forth,
Rare in color, outlandish in sound.
    And then,
When the three lights, sun, moon, and stars, shine clear
And heaven and earth are everywhere illumined,
Then, without troubling Marquis Yang for passage,
One may mount on magic footsteps, break clean away,
To visit An-ch'i on the island of P'eng-lai,
To view the emperor's form as it was on Mount Ch'iao.4
In the distance faintly visible, troops of immortals
Feast on jade by the clear-watered shore,
Shod in sandals left behind at Fu-hsiang,
Robed in drooping feathers and plumes.
They soar by the ponds of Heaven,

---

4 Marquis Yang is the god of the waves. An-ch'i is an immortal spirit living on
the magic island of P'eng-lai. A native of a place called Fu-hsiang, he left his
sandals there when he went off to become an immortal, a fact referred to below.
Mount Ch'iao is the place where the Yellow Emperor left his hat and robe when
he ascended into the sky to become an immortal.

Go sporting to the farthest darkness,
Showing what it means to have a body but no desires,
To keep living on and on to the end of time.
    These are the sea's capacities:
To enfold the heart of the *ch'ien* trigram,
Encompass all the realms of the *k'un*;5
A house for spirits,
Domicile of gods,
What rarity not found within it,
What wonder not in store?
Abundant the waters that gather there;
It accepts their forms, remaining empty within.
Far-flung, the virtue of the trigram *k'an*,
Choosing the lowliest place to dwell!
It enhances what goes forth, receives what comes,
Their ancestor, their metropolis;
Of all things and creatures, all species alive,
What does it possess, what does it not?

5 *Ch'ien* and *k'un* are the trigrams of Heaven and Earth respectively in the
I Ching or *Book of Changes; k'an*, referred to seven lines below, represents water.

SUN CH'O

4TH CEN.

☙

WANDERING ON MOUNT T'IEN-T'AI

Sun Ch'o, serving as governor of Yung-chia on the coast of present-day Chekiang, conceived a strong desire to resign from office and retire to Mount T'ien-t'ai, situated north of Yung-chia. He is said to have had maps or diagrams of the mountain drawn for him; and in the poem that follows, he realizes his desire by performing the ascent of the mountain in imagination. As he proceeds up the mountain, the scenery becomes increasingly fantastic and idealized, until at the end he reaches a plane of pure philosophy, in which Taoist and Buddhist allusions are carefully balanced one against the other. Wen hsüan 11.

☙

MOUNT T'IEN-T'AI is the sacred flower of all mountain ranges. Cross the sea and you will find Fang-chang and P'eng-lai; turn inland and you will come to Ssu-ming and T'ien-t'ai, all of them places where the sages of the occult wander and perform their transformations, where the holy immortals have their caves and dwellings.[1] The endlessly soaring shapes of these ranges, their miraculous beauty exhaust the wealth and wonder of mountain and sea, embrace all that is brave and admirable among gods and men. The reason that Mount T'ien-t'ai is not ranked among the Five Sacred Peaks, that records of it are lacking in the classical texts—is it not that it stands in such a remote and out-of-the-way place, that the road there is

[1] Fang-chang and P'eng-lai, as we have seen in the previous selection, are mythical mountains in the eastern sea, the home of immortal spirits; Ssu-ming is just north of the T'ien-t'ai range.

so long and hard to trace? Now casting its shadow into the many-fathomed depths, now hiding its summit among a thousand ranges—to reach it one must first travel the path of goblins and trolls, and finally enter the realm where no human being lives. Few men in all the world have ever succeeded in climbing it; no kings have come to offer sacrifices. Therefore mention of it is not to be found in ordinary writings; its name is celebrated only in the accounts of wonders.

And yet the diagram of the mountain that has been drawn for me—how could it be a deception? Surely if one is not the kind who will abandon the world to amuse himself with the Way, who will give up grain to subsist on a diet of mushrooms, then how can he hope to clamber nimbly up its slopes and make his home there? If one is not the sort who can embark on a far-off journey in order to delve into mysteries, who is fervent in his faith and can make his spirit go where he wishes, then how would he dare attempt to visit it in distant imagination?

And so it is that I have caused my spirit to gallop and my thoughts to turn round and round, chanting by day and watching by night, until, in less time than it takes to wag one's head, it seems as though I have already twice ascended the mountain! Now I am about to cast off all bonds and shackles and reside forever on these peaks. But because I cannot bear to go on forever with these mumbled imaginings, I have called upon literature to aid me in expressing what is in my heart.

The Great Void, vast and wide, that knows no boundary,
Sets in cycle the mysterious Being, So-of-itself;[2]
Melting, it forms the rivers and waterways;
Thickening, it turns into mountains and hills.
Ah, the awesome eminence of T'ien-t'ai's peak—
Truly it must be held up by the gods!
Under the Herdboy's protection, it flaunts its bright crests;
Sheltering in the holy land of Yüeh, it makes certain of a four-
          square base,[3]

[2] The So-of-itself (tzu-jan) is another name for the Way.

[3] The Herdboy star is thought to protect the region of Yüeh, where Mount T'ien-t'ai is situated.

Spreading a net of roots vaster than mounts Hua and Tai,
Pointing straight upward, taller than the Nine Doubts,
Equal of the "counterpart of Heaven" in the "Canon of Yao,"
A match for the "craggy heights" of the Odes of Chou.
Yet so far away are those peerless regions,
So remote and mysterious,
That the petty-wise merely gaze but fail to journey there,
And those who go, because the trail runs out, never find the way.
I laugh at such summer insects who doubt that ice exists,[4]
Prepare my light-winged mount, longing to depart.
No inner law stays forever hidden and undisclosed:
See how these two wonders parade their form!
Red Wall, like sunset mists ascending, planted for a guidepost,[5]
The Cataract, leaping and plunging, to blazon the way.
When I glimpse these sacred signs, then I will be off;
Suddenly now I am on my way,
Asking the feathered men on their cinnabar hills[6]
How to find that happy domain where no one ever dies.
If the heights of T'ien-t'ai can really be scaled,
Why long for the Storied City?[7]
I'll cast off the constant attachments of this world,
Giving vent to nobler, more exalted feelings;
Clad in shaggy folds of fur and felt,
With the clang-clang of the metal staff I wield,
I'll push through the murk of tangled forests,
Climb the sharp acclivity of precipice and slope,
Across Yu Creek and straight ahead,
Moving quickly past the point where five counties join.
Then straddling the arc of the soaring stone bridge,
I'll peer down ten thousand feet to untold depths;
I'll tread the slippery moss-covered stone,

---

[4] *Chuang Tzu* 17: "You can't discuss ice with a summer insect—he's bound to a single season."

[5] The road up T'ien-t'ai, we are told, led off from a rise called Red Wall.

[6] The immortal spirits.

[7] The city of God in the fabulous K'un-lun Mountains of the far west.

Reach for the cliff that rises like a kingfisher-colored screen,
Snatch the strands of dodder that trail from tall trees,
Cling to the flying stems of creeper and vine.
But though I face a moment's danger, on the brink of a fall,
In the end I gain forever the gift of long life.
So long as I keep faith with the dark and hidden Way,
I may trudge the steepest slopes and they are level plains to me;
And when I have traversed all their nine turnings,
The road will stretch before me unending and clear,
Where my heart will wander unconcerned, my eyes roam free,
And I will let my slow steps take me where they will.
I'll spread a mat of slender grasses, rich and tender,
Sheltering beneath those lanky giants, the tall pines;
Watch the flight of winging *luan* birds,
Listen to the chorus of phoenixes warbling.
And when I've crossed Spirit Gorge and bathed myself there,
All the nagging worries will be cleansed from my chest;
In the swirling flow I'll wash away the last fleck of "dust,"
Free myself from the pursuing darkness of the "five
            becloudings";[8]
Then I'll set out to follow the matchless ways of Fu-hsi and
            Shen-nung,
To tread in the dark footsteps of the two named Lao.[9]
Clambering up and down, camping a night or two,
I'll come at last to the city of immortals,
Its double gates like banks of cloud flanking the road,
Its garnet terrace thrust halfway to the sky, suspended there;
Vermilion portals glowing and resplendent among the trees,
Jade halls now hidden, now bright on the tall turn of the hill,
With rosy clouds arrayed like wings at lattice casements,
The radiant sun streaming through window grilles.

---

[8] According to Buddhist doctrine there are six "dusts" that defile the mind:
form, sound, smell, taste, touch, and perception of characteristics; the "five
becloudings" which darken the mind are desire, anger, drowsiness, excitability,
and doubt.

[9] Fu-hsi and Shen-nung are mythical cultural heroes of antiquity; the "two
named Lao" are Lao Tzu and Lao Lai Tzu, Taoist sages.

Eight huge cassia trees stand high and unscarred by frost,
Five-hued mushrooms unfold their caps in the morning light.
Gentle breezes pile up fragrance in the sunny woods;
Spring water, sweet to the taste, bubbles through shady channels.
The *chien* tree rises a thousand yards without casting a shadow;
The *ch'i*-gem tree, sparkling and shining, droops with jewels.
Wang Ch'iao, a crane for his mount, hurries up to heaven;
The "responders-to-Truth," waving their staffs, pace the void,[10]
Performing the hocus-pocus of their uncanny transformations,
Suddenly emerging from Being to enter Non-being.
       And then,
When I have come full circle in my wandering inspection,
Body stilled, mind at rest,
When whatever "hurts the horses" has been done away with,[11]
And chores of the world all have been renounced,
Then, wherever I move my knife, it will always find the hollow;
I'll eye the ox but never see it whole.[12]
Composing my thoughts beside the somber cliffs,
I'll chant in a clear voice by the endless river.
       And so,
When Hsi-ho, charioteer of the sun, arrives at the point of noon,
And trailing vapors have lifted and dispersed,
The dharma-drums, booming, will wake the echoes,
And countless blends of incense send up pungent smoke,
In preparation for audience with the Heavenly Ancestor,[13]
For the gathering here of the enrolled immortals.
We will dip up the rich oil of black jade,

[10] Wang Ch'iao is a Taoist immortal; the "responders-to-Truth" are Buddhist saints.

[11] A reference to *Chuang Tzu* 24, the anecdote in which the Yellow Emperor asks a young herder of horses how to govern the empire. The boys replies, "Governing the empire I suppose is not much different from herding horses. Get rid of whatever is harmful to the horses—that's all."

[12] A reference to *Chuang Tzu* 3, which describes the remarkable butcher who moved his carving knife through the natural hollows of the ox's body, and no longer "saw the whole ox."

[13] Some identify the Heavenly Ancestor as Lao Tzu, though the term may refer to the sun, moon, and other heavenly bodies, or to deities in general.

Freshen our mouths in the springs of Flower Lake,
Spreading doctrines of what is "beyond symbol,"
Expounding texts on what is "without origination";[14]
Till we realize that Being can never wholly be rejected,
That to walk with Non-being still leaves gaps.[15]
We'll destroy both Form and Emptiness, making our path one,
Turn at once to Being, and thereby gain the Way,
Abandoning the two "names" that spring from a single source,
Wiping out the one nothingness of the "three banners."[16]
Then we may chatter as merrily as we like all day long—
It will be the same as utter silence, as though we'd never spoken.
We will merge the ten thousand images through deepest
          contemplation;
Unwitting, we'll join our bodies with the So-of-itself.

[14] The lines refer to Taoism and Buddhism respectively.

[15] Both Taoism and Buddhism teach the student, as a step in his training, to give up concepts of being and purposive action and embrace those of nothingness and non-action; but true enlightenment comes when he can transcend such dualistic thinking and accept things as they exist. The remainder of the poem plays in paradoxical terms on these ideas of transcendence and acceptance.

[16] The two "names" are the named and the nameless (Taoist doctrine); the "three banners" are identified as form, the voidness of form, and meditation (Buddhist doctrine), though the exact meaning of the term is very uncertain. See the translation of this poem by Richard B. Mather, "The Mystical Ascent of the T'ient'ai Mountains: Sun Ch'o's *Yu-T'ien-t'ai-shan Fu*."

ॐ

THE SNOW

The "Fu on the Snow" by Hsieh Hui-lien, cousin of the famous landscape poet Hsieh Ling-yün, appears to be a work of pure literary fiction, with no overt references to the writer's own time or personality. It is set in what was looked upon as one of the golden ages of fu *writing, the time of the early Han nobleman King Hsiao of Liang, the other great age being that of Sung Yü and his patron, King Hsiang of Ch'u, depicted in the "Fu on the Wind." Ssu-ma Hsiang-ju is portrayed as the author of the main parts of the work, with the poets Tsou Yang and Mei Sheng contributing two songs in a slightly different meter and a reprise, while the snow itself speaks the concluding words. In Hsieh Hui-lien's treatment, the snow becomes not merely a natural phenomenon to be described objectively, but a source of joy, an object of aesthetic appreciation, and, like the wind of Sung Yü's poem, a symbolic presence capable of conveying lessons of deep moral and philosophical import.* Wen hsüan 13.

ॐ

THE YEAR WAS ENDING, the season in its twilight; cold winds piled up and cheerless clouds filled the sky. The king of Liang, dispirited, wandered in the Rabbit Garden; then he laid out choice wine and sent for his guests and companions, a summons to Master Tsou, an invitation to Uncle Mei; Ssu-ma Hsiang-ju arrived last, taking the place of honor to the right of the other guests.¹ All at once a fine sleet began to fall, followed by heavy snow. The king proceeded to intone the "North Wind" from the songs of Wei, and to hum the "Southern Mountain" from the odes of Chou.² Then, offering a writing tablet to Lord Ssu-ma, he said, "Try delving into your secret thoughts, setting your sleekest words to galloping; match color for color, weigh your fine effects, and make me a *fu* on this scene!"

Ssu-ma Hsiang-ju moved politely off his mat, rose, retreated a few steps, and bowed. "I have heard," he said, "that the Snow Palace was constructed in an eastern country, that the Snow Mountain soars in a western borderland. Ch'ang of Ch'i poured out his lament of 'when we come back'; Man of the Chi clan fashioned his song on the yellow bamboo.³ The Ts'ao air employs hemp robes as a simile for its color; Ch'u singers pair the Hidden Orchid with the song about it.⁴ If it piles up a foot deep, it offers fair omen for a rich year ahead; but more than ten feet, it signals disharmony besetting the power of the yin. The snow has far-reaching significance where the seasons are concerned. With your permission, I'll speak of how it all begins:

When the dark months have run out
And harsh breaths are ascendant;

---

¹ Liu Wu, posthumously known as King Hsiao of Liang, was a younger brother of Emperor Ching (r. 157–141 B.C.) of the Former Han. The Rabbit Garden, where he and his guests took part in cultured pastimes, is famous in literary history. The poets referred to here are Tsou Yang (2d cen. B.C.), Mei Sheng (d. 140 B.C.), and Ssu-ma Hsiang-ju (179–117 B.C.).

² *Book of Odes* #41 and #210, both songs having to do in part with snow.

³ Ch'ang, posthumously known as King Wen of Chou, is supposed to have written the song in *Odes* #167 which contains the lines: "Long ago we set out/ when willows were rich and green./ Now we come back/ through thickly falling snow." Man is the personal name of King Mu of Chou, who wrote the Yellow Bamboo song at a time of severe cold. In characteristic Chinese fashion, Ssu-ma Hsiang-ju begins with a barrage of classical allusions before settling down to the actual description.

⁴ *Odes* #150, one of the airs of the state of Ts'ao, compares the whiteness of snow to that of hemp robes; Hidden Orchid and White Snow are two pieces often performed by singers and lute players of the state of Ch'u.

When Scorching Creek ices over,
And Hot Water Valley freezes,
The Well of Fire is quenched
And Warm Springs congeal,
Their bubbling pools no longer churning,
Their fiery winds having ceased to stir;
When north-facing doorways have been chinked with plaster
And the land of the naked swathes itself in cloth;
Then rivers and seas bring forth clouds,
Northern deserts send their sands flying,
Wreathing vapor to vapor, piling up mists,
Hiding the sun, engulfing its red rays.
Sleet is the first to come hissing down,
Followed by thicker and thicker flurries of snow;
See them darting, scattering, mingling, turning,
Blanketing, blinding, dense and dark,
Softly seething, bobbing, gliding,
Faster and faster falling now,
Endless wings that beat and flutter,
Swirling till they come to rest in drifts.
At first they light on roof tiles, crowning the ridgepole;
In the end they force the blinds apart, slither in through cracks;
Where earlier they sidled nimbly over porch and verandah,
Now they whirl and tumble by curtain and mat.
In square hollows they form jade pilasters,
In round holes they're transformed into circlets of jade.
Mark the lowlands—ten thousand acres of the same fabric;
Look at the mountains—a thousand cliffs all white!
Now terraces become like stacked jade discs,
Highways like ribbons of alabaster;
Courtyards are fitted with flights of jasper steps,
Forests ranged with chalcedony trees.
The snowy crane is robbed of distinction,
The silver pheasant bereft of hue;
Silken sleeves find their beauty shamefully lacking,
Jade faces hide their fairness from sight.
While the heaps of whiteness have not yet melted,

And the bright sun of morning shines clear,
They gleam like the Torch Dragon,
Flame in mouth, that illumines the K'un-lun Mountains;
And when rivulets flow and drip down in icicles,
Dangling from gutters, hanging at roof corners,
They sparkle as though P'ing-i, god of rivers,
Had pried open mussels and hung out bright pearls.
Such is this show of tangled profusion,
This model of stainlessness, purity, white;
The force of this wheeling, staggering onrush,
The wonder of this dazzle and charge,
That its shifting forms seem never to end—
Ah, who can hope to understand them all!
Before I finish, shall I describe our pastimes?
The night, dark and still, wakes many thoughts.
Wind buffets the columns, its echoes tumbling;
Moonlight rests on curtains, its rays pouring through.
We dip rich wine brewed from Hsiang waters in Wu,
Don double capes of fox and badger,
Face the garden pheasants that dance in pairs,
Watch the cloud-borne goose winging alone.
And as I walk the drifts of mingled sleet and snow,
I pity these leaves and branches forced apart;
Distant thoughts race a thousand miles away,
I long to join hands and go home together."[5]

Tsou Yang, hearing these words, was moved by pity and admiration and, thinking to add to the beautiful flow of sound, he respectfully asked if he might contribute a composition of his own. Then he rose to his feet and recited this "Song of the Drifted Snow":

"Join hands, my lovely,
Lift the folded curtains,
Spread silken comforters,
Perfumed mats to sit on.
We'll light up incense burners,

[5] According to commentators, the leaves and branches remind the poet of his brothers and kinsmen far away and he longs to join them.

Make the torches glow,
Ladle cassia-scented wine
To sing this pure refrain."

Continuing, he composed the "Song of the White Snow":

"Songs have been sung,
Wine already drunk;
Red faces flushed now,
Thoughts must turn to love.
I want to let down the curtains, push the pillows close;
I dream of untying sashes, of loosing girdle bands.
I hate the year so quickly ended,
Grieve we have no means to meet again.
Only see the white snow on the stairs—
How little will be left to shine in the warmth of spring!"

When he had finished, the king tried singing the songs over to himself two or three times, getting the feel of them, waving his arm to keep time. Then, turning to Mei Sheng, he asked him to stand up and compose a Reprise. This is how it went:

White feathers too are white,
But lightness is their special nature;[6]
White jade too is white,
But stubbornly it guards the chaste hardness of its form.
Neither can match this snow
That comes into being and melts away with the season.
When the dark yin freezes, its purity stays unsullied,
But when the warm sun shines, it no longer strives to guard its virtue:

"Virtue—when was that my fame?
Purity—what concern of mine?
Riding the clouds, I soar and descend,
Tagging the wind, I tumble and fall,
Taking on the form of things I encounter,

---

[6] Lightness would also seem to be a characteristic of snow; but I think Hsieh has in mind the contrast between an accumulation of feathers, which is still relatively light, and an accumulation of snow, which is much heavier than one would anticipate from watching it fall.

Assuming the shape of the land where I lie.
I'm white when that which I touch is so,
Grimy when surroundings stain me.
Free, my heart wanders far and wide;
What is there to fret over, what is there to plan?"

DESOLATE CITY

*The poem deals with the city of Kuang-ling, situated north of the Yangtze,
not far from its mouth, in present-day Kiangsu. A canal, linking the
Yangtze to the Huai River in the north, runs by its side. It saw its first great
period of glory in Former Han times as capital of the state of Wu when Liu
P'i, the king of Wu, grew rich by boiling sea water to extract salt and
minting cash from the copper ore in its mountains. In 154 B.C., Liu P'i led
six other feudal states in an abortive revolt against the supreme ruler,
Emperor Ching, which quickly ended in disaster. Much later, in A.D. 459,
another feudal lord with his base in Kuang-ling raised a rebellion against the
Sung dynasty, but was soon crushed, his city destroyed, and over three
thousand of its inhabitants massacred. The poet-official Pao Chao, visiting the
area shortly after, recalls the former wealth and grandeur of the city and
laments its present sad condition. It is said that he intended his poem as a
warning to yet another leader who was embarking upon a course of rebellion.
Wen hsüan 11.*

Broad and far-reaching, the level plain,
Hurrying south to Ts'ang-wu and the Sea of Chang,
Racing north to Purple Barriers, the Wild Goose Gate,
Its barge canal like a tow rope to haul it about,
Its K'un-lun of hills to serve as an axle,
A fastness of double rivers, of many-fold passes,

A corridor where four roads meet, where five pass through.
Long ago, at the time of its greatest prospering,
Carriages clashed axle heads,
Men jostled shoulders,
House rows and alley gates crowded the earth,
Songs and piping shrilled to the sky.
There was wealth to be wrung from fields of salt,
Profit to be pared from copper mountains;
Its talented and strong ones grew rich and mighty,
Its horses and riders were handsome and well trained.
So it could flout the laws of Ch'in,
Overstep the regulations of Chou,
Troweling smooth its lofty battlements,
Channeling out the deepest moats,
Hoping to prolong its generations with the help of fair fortune.
    Thus
Pounded earth was raised to form a forest of parapets,
An awesome file of turrets and beacon towers,
Taller in measure than the Five Mountains,
Broader across than the Three Dikes,
Precipitous as a sheer escarpment,
Rising straight up like a bank of long clouds.
They were fitted with magnets to guard against assault,[1]
Daubed with russet clay to lend the fancy of design.
Gazing on the firmness of those gates and bastions,
You'd think one lord could hold them for ten thousand years;
Yet now, when three dynasties have come and gone,[2]
Five hundred years and more have passed,
They lie split like melons, like bean pods broken open.

Damp mosses cling to the well,
Tangles of kudzu vine snare the path;
Halls are laced with vipers and crawling things,
Musk deer and flying squirrel quarrel by the stairs.

[1] The gates of ancient cities were said to have been fitted with loadstones to detect weapons concealed on those who entered.

[2] The Han, Wei, and Chin.

Tree goblin and mountain sprite,
Field rat, fox in the wall
Howl at the wind, whimper in the rain,
At dusk appearing, scampering off at dawn.
Hungry falcons whet their beaks,
Cold hawks hiss at those who menace their chicks;
Lurking tigers, crouching cats
Suck blood and dine on flesh.
Thickets of fallen trees clog the road,
The old thoroughfare, deep and overgrown;
White poplars shed their leaves early,
Bleak grasses withered long ago;
Breath of frost, keen and biting;
Soo, soo, the bullying of the wind:
A lone tumbleweed trembles by itself,
Puffs of sand for no reason suddenly start up.
Dense copses murky and unending,
A jungle of weeds and brush leaning on each other;
The circling moat caved in long ago,
Towering battlements—they too have tumbled:
One looks straight out a thousand li or more,
Seeing only the whirls of yellow dust.
　　Dwell on it, listen in silence—
　　It wounds the heart, breaking it in two.
　　And so
The painted doors, the gaily stitched hangings,
Sites where once were halls of song, pavilions of the dance,
Jasper pools, trees of jadeite,
Lodges for those who hunt in woods, who fish the shores,
Music of Wu, Ts'ai, Ch'i, Ch'in,
Vessels in shapes of fish and dragon, sparrow and horse—
All have lost their incense, gone to ash,
Their radiance engulfed, their echoes cut off.
Mysterious princess from the Eastern Capital,
Beautiful lady from a southern land,
With heart of orchis, limbs of white lawn,
Marble features, carmine lip—

None whose soul is not entombed in somber stone,
Whose bones do not lie dwindling in the dust.
Do you recall now what joy it was to share your lord's carriage?
The pain of being banished to a palace apart?
Is it Heaven's way
To make so many taste sorrow?
Bring the lute—I will sing,
Fashioning a song of the Desolate City.
    The song says:

    Border winds hurrying
    Above the castle cold.
    Well and pathway gone from sight,
    Hill and grave mound crumbling.
    A thousand years,
      Ten thousand ages,
    All end thus—
      What is there to say?

CHIANG YEN
444–505

PARTINGS

The poet-official Chiang Yen is famous for two fu, *included in* Wen hsüan 16, *that have as their object the depiction of certain emotions. One, the* Hen fu *or "Fu on Grievances," describes a number of men and women in history who were forced to endure some grief or injustice. The other, the* Pieh fu *or "Fu on Partings," is presented here. Like the* Hen fu, *it lacks any prose introduction or formal closing. Plunging immediately into the subject, it begins with an exclamation on the terrible sadness of parting, and then elaborates by presenting a series of vignettes depicting various types of parting and separation. Among these are the partings at the farewell parties of the wealthy nobles, the parting that takes place when a swordsman bids good-by to his family to go off on a mission of vengeance, when a son departs for war, when a traveler sets off for remote lands, when an official is obliged to leave his wife because of government service, or when a recluse makes his final withdrawal from the mundane world. The language of the descriptions is highly polished and ornate, and not without its effectiveness, though one misses in the poem any expression of the poet's own feelings such as is found in the more personal works of earlier* fu *writers.*

The very soul seems to dissolve in darkness—
Only parting can afflict us so!
Worse when the land is as far as Ch'in from Wu,
The thousand miles that separate Yen from Sung;

At a season when spring mosses have just begun growing,
Or autumn breezes suddenly spring up!
Then the journeyer's heart is wounded
By a hundred stabs of woe and grief.
The wind whines and whistles with an unfamiliar cry,
The endless banks of clouds take on strange hues;
His boat lingers falteringly beside the river bank,
His carriage moves with halting slowness by the border of the hill.
Oars are unplied—what heart has he to go forward?
Horses neigh unceasingly, a melancholy sound.
The traveler puts down the golden wine cup—who is there to urge
          him?
Pushes aside the jade-fretted lute, tears wetting carriage bars.
The one left behind lies disconsolate,
Vacant-minded, as though bereft,
As the sun sinks behind the wall, muting its colors,
And the moon climbs above the eaves to cast its rays abroad;
Watching the crimson orchid drenched in dew,
Gazing far off at green catalpas touched by frost,
Threading among tall columns, vainly wiping away the tears,
Fingering the brocade curtains, lost in hopeless sorrow,
Knowing how the traveler's footsteps must falter in dreams of
          parting,
How his soul at separation must be wandering far and wide.
     Partings evoke but a single emotion,
Though they take ten thousand forms:
Those of the dragon-horsed, the silver-saddled,[1]
Who ride in red coaches with gaudy painted hubs,
Rigging screens and drinking at the gate to the Eastern Capital,
Seeing guests off in Golden Valley,[2]
When lutes are tuned to the *yü* mode, flutes and drums set out,
With songs of Yen and Chao to make the lovely ladies sad,

[1] Dragon horses are steeds of exceptionally fine quality and size. This passage describes the partings and farewell parties of the rich aristocrats.

[2] The gate to the Eastern Capital, in Ch'ang-an, and Golden Valley, near Lo-yang, were places where the wealthy officials Shu Kuang (1st cen. B.C.) and Shih Ch'ung (249–300) respectively held their farewell parties.

Pearls and jade lustrous in the last days of autumn,
Gauzes and chiffons shimmering in early spring,
Enough to startle teams of four, make them look up from feed
        troughs,
To rouse the fish from deep springs, coax them to show their
        scales.
But when the hour comes to let go hands, to choke back the tears,
All sink into deep silence, spirits slain with grief.

    Again there are swordsmen, ashamed of kindness unrepaid,
Young men whose mission is revenge,
From the state of Han, the privy of Chao,
The palace of Wu, the market place of Yen,3
Severing ties of affection, turning their backs on love,
Leaving homeland and village behind,
Weeping as they say good-by,
Wiping tears of blood when they look their last,
Spurring their journey-bound horses with no backward glance,
Eyes fixed on the dust of the road that whirls up from time to time.
Gratitude prompts them to offer their single swords,
Not the hope of some reward to be gained beyond the grave,
Though metal and stone fright them and their faces pale,
Though flesh and blood mourn them to the very heart's death.4

    Perhaps in border provinces peace has yet to come,
And one must shoulder feathered arrows, join the troops,
Beside Liao waters that know no end,
To Yen Mountain, tall among the clouds.

---

3 References to Nieh Cheng, Yü Jang, Chuan Chu, and Ching K'o, men whose lives are recorded in the "Biographies of the Assassin-Retainers," *Shih chi* 86 (see my translation in *Records of the Historian: Chapters from the Shih chi of Ssu-ma Ch'ien* [Columbia University Press, 1969], pp. 45–67). All left their homes and loved ones in an attempt to carry out revenge for their rulers or patrons.

4 The previous line refers to Wu Yang, one of the assassins mentioned in *Shih chi* 86, who with Ching K'o made an attempt on the life of the First Emperor of the Ch'in. At the last minute, when faced with the emperor and his court musicians playing on instruments of metal and stone, Wu Yang turned pale with fear. The second line refers to Nieh Cheng, described in the same chapter, whose sister mourned over his corpse, though it cost her her life.

In women's chambers, breezes are warm;
Along the roadside, grasses smell sweet;
The sun comes out in the heavens, its bright beams shining;
Dew settles to the ground, making contours spring to life;
Light mirrored in the splendor of vermilion ceilings,
Odor mingled with a smoldering haze of blue-misted incense: 5
Plucking branches of peach and plum, they cannot bear to part,
Sending off this beloved son, gauze skirts wet with tears.

    To set out once and for all for lands far away—
Who knows when we'll meet again?
Gazing at the tall trees of the old home town,
Taking leave by the northern bridge, a long good-by,
Those to left and right all deeply moved,
Kin and companions bathed in tears.
Let us spread rushes, speak our regret;
Wine casks alone will help us voice this sorrow.
Now in the days when autumn geese are winging,
Here in the season when white dew falls,
Grieve and grieve again past the bend of the distant mountain,
Going farther and farther away beside the long river's rim!

    Perhaps a husband sojourns right of the river Tzu,
His wife at home, south of the Yellow River.
Once their girdlestones glinted side by side in morning radiance;
They shared the evening perfume of a golden stove.
Then he donned official seals, went a thousand miles away,
Sad to leave his precious flower, her fragrance wasted.
In deep rooms she lacks the heart to tune up lute or zither,
Darkens her high tower with drapes of yellow silk.
Spring rooms are closed to green mossy colors,
Autumn curtains let in the bright moon's beams;
Summer mats are chill through days that know no twilight;
Winter lamps glare through nights so terribly long!
Song of the woven brocade—tears are all cried out;

---

5 Many interpretations are offered for these obscure lines. At this point the young man setting off to war, who is the subject of this paragraph, all but disappears from sight as the poet focuses on those whom he leaves behind.

Poems of the acrostic—her shadow pining alone.[6]
　　Here a man, more than ordinary, in the shade of Mount Hua,
Swallows pills to gain the rank of immortal;
His art already marvelous, still he studies;
His way one of quietude, though there's more for him to learn;
Close by his furnace, he no longer thinks of the world;
Smelting cinnabar in golden caldrons, his will now firmly fixed.
Crane-borne, he will climb to the heavens,
Drawn by *luan* birds, ascend the sky,
Where ten thousand miles are the briefest journey,
A thousand years no more than a moment's separation.
Yet so gravely the world looks on partings,
It cannot take leave of him without lingering regret.
　　On less exalted levels, we have the peony poem,
The song of the lovely maiden,
Of the Wei girl from Sang-chung,
The Ch'in beauty from Shang-kuan.[7]
Over spring grasses jade-green in hue,
By spring waters whose ripples run clear,
I saw you off at Southern Cove—
It hurt, but what could I do?
Or later, when autumn dewdrops were like pearls,
And the autumn moon seemed a circlet of jade.
Bright moons, white dew—
They shine and darken, come and go;
Yet each time I part from you,
My fond heart is restless and distraught!
　　So it is that parting knows no fixed form;
Patterns of parting bear a thousand names.
But where there's parting there will surely be regret,
And where there are regrets they must overflow,

[6] Reference to Su Hui (4th cen.), whose husband, Tou T'ao, took another wife while away on official travel. In reproach she composed an acrostic poem which she executed in brocade and sent to him. The acrostic consists of a square measuring twenty-nine characters to a side which, by reading in various directions, may be made to yield over two hundred poems.

[7] The references are to love songs in the *Book of Odes* and other early collections of poetry.

Making men dazed in mind, stricken in spirit,
Broken-hearted, pierced to the bone.
Though I possessed the matchless ink of Wang Pao or Yang
        Hsiung,
The deft brushes of Yen An and Hsü Yüeh,
All the finest writers of the Golden Chamber,
Numberless masters of the Orchid Terrace,
Whose rhyme-prose is said to lift one soaring over clouds,
Whose eloquence earns the name of dragon-carving,[8]
Who could describe the form of these temporary partings,
Who could catch the likeness of these long farewells?

[8] Wang Pao and the other writers mentioned are all famous Han literary figures; the Golden Chamber and Orchid Terrace are Han government offices associated with literary activities. Soaring over the clouds is a reference to Ssu-ma Hsiang-ju (see Introduction p. 2); "dragon-carving" is a phrase employed to describe the eloquence of an earlier figure, the philosopher Tsou Shih (4th cen. B.C.).

A SMALL GARDEN

Yü Hsin, born of an aristocratic family that had distinguished itself in literature and statesmanship, early became an official at the court of the Liang dynasty, which had its capital in the south at present-day Nanking. After the rebellion of Hou Ching that broke out in 548, temporarily disrupting the life of the dynasty, he was dispatched as envoy to the Western Wei, one of the non-Chinese dynasties that ruled in the north. While he was there, the northerners launched an attack on the Liang and Yü Hsin, forcibly detained, was obliged to stand by and watch the destruction of his home state. The following poem was written when he was living, a virtual captive, in Ch'ang-an, the northern capital, probably shortly after the attack on the Liang in the winter of 554. In it, he describes in great detail the small garden of the house where he and his family live, as though determined to convince himself that he is in fact living the life of a wise and carefree recluse. But his thoughts in time turn to the past—his privileged youth, the grim days of the Hou Ching rebellion, and the even more tragic times that followed—and he ends by pouring out his longing for his homeland and his feelings of guilt and despair. The Western Wei and its successor, the Northern Chou, though showering official position and honor upon Yü Hsin, would never permit him to go home, and he died an alien in the north in 581.

Yü Hsin's poetry is admired not only for its graceful diction and technical skill but for the depth of feeling that informs much of it, particularly that written when he was under detention in the north. As will be apparent from the work that follows, he restored to the rhyme-prose form a note of intense personal emotion. At the same time the passion for allusions had by his day so infected the style of both poetry and prose that his poem, for all

*its sincerity and pathos, all but sinks under the weight of them. The text is
found in* Yü Tzu-shan chi, *ch.* 1.

On one branch alone
The Nest Father could find a spot to nest in safety;
In one single pot
The Pot Gentleman discovered room for his whole body.[1]
Or better, Kuan Ning's sofa of goosefoot vine,
Poked full of holes but still good for sitting;
Or Hsi K'ang's smelting oven—
When firing was finished, it served for a nap.[2]
What need for rows of doorways, chamber beyond chamber,
Mansions like that of Fan Chung of Nan-yang;
For green porches, blue latticework,
Homes like that of Wang Ken of the Western Han?
I have a few acres, a shabby hut,
Lonely and still, beyond the world of men,
Enough to fend off the worst of summer and winter,
Enough to shelter me from wind and frost.
Though I'm closer to the market than Yen Ying was,
I don't send morning and evening to ask about the bargains;[3]
Like P'an Yüeh, I face the city,
Savoring delights of an idle life.[4]
The yellow crane, alarmed at the first frost,
Has no wish for wheels or a carriage;

[1] The Nest Father was a recluse of high antiquity who lived in a tree, the Pot
Gentleman a sage of the Eastern Han who slept in a large pot suspended in his
otherwise bare room.

[2] Kuan Ning was a recluse; Hsi K'ang, who in his poorer days was supposed to
have made a living by smelting iron, has appeared on p. 61.

[3] Yen Ying (d. 500 B.C.), a statesman noted for his frugality, was urged by his
sovereign to move out of the crowded part of the city to a pleasanter neighbor-
hood, but he replied that he preferred living close to the market place so he
could send over morning and evening to buy what happened to be cheap.

[4] On P'an Yüeh, see p. 64.

The *yuan-chü* bird, fleeing the wind,
Is wholly uninterested in bells and drums.5
In Lu Chi's case, two brothers roomed together;
In Han K'ang's, uncle and nephew managed not to part;6
A snail's horn, a mosquito's eyelash,
Still offer space enough to fit into!
    And so
The wine cellar's where I linger;
I too have knocked a hole in the wall.7
Among the paulownias, dew drips down;
Under the willows, a breeze begins to stir.
My lute is the kind with pegs of pearl;
My book bears the title "Cup of Jade."8
I have crabapples but no hall of that name,
Sour jujubes, though no towers to match.9
But still there's room to zigzag eighty or ninety feet,
To walk up and down many tens of paces.
Elms and willows, two or three rows of them,
Pears and peaches, a stand of over a hundred:
Part the dense foliage and you'll find a window,
Thread in and out among them and come on a path;
Dense cover for cicadas—they never take alarm;

5 Duke Yi of Wei sought to please his pet crane by taking it for a ride in a carriage. The sea bird called *yuan-chü* took refuge from a storm in the capital city of Lu where, to the bird's distress, the inhabitants offered it sacrifices and serenaded it with bells and drums. Yü Hsin hints that he hopes the rulers of the northern dynasty will not try to force him to take office under them.

6 Lu Chi, author of the "*Fu* on Literature," in his youth shared cramped and humble quarters with his younger brother Yün when, after the destruction of their native state of Wu, they came north to seek their fortune. Han K'ang faithfully followed his maternal uncle Yin Hao in a life of enforced wandering. Yü Hsin likens himself to these displaced wanderers.

7 When Yen Ho was pressed by the ruler of Lu to appear for an interview, he knocked a hole in the rear wall of his garden and ran away.

8 Actually a chapter from a very serious work of philosophy by the Han Confucian Tung Chung-shu; Yü Hsin mentions it here only because it forms such a neat parallel to the "pegs of pearl" in the line above.

9 Crabapple and Sour Jujube are the names, respectively, of a famous hall and pair of towers.

No nets spread for the pheasant—what has he to fear?
Plants and trees tangled and untrained,
Stalks and branches twined together;
For hills a heap of shoveled-up earth,
In the ground, a tiny hollow for a pond;
Secretive wildcats burrow side by side,
Fledgling magpies nest together.
Delicate grasses, seeds strung like pearls,
Cool gourds dangling from their long handles—
These can mend the pangs of hunger,
These can offer comfort and rest.
Crooked and sagging are my narrow rooms,
Worn and leaky, my roof of thatch:
Under the eaves try to straighten up—they knock your hat off;
Walk through the door in the usual way and get a thump on the
   brow.
Roosting by my curtain are no white cranes,
Though tortoises hold up the legs of my couch.[10]
Birds throng my quiet days,
Flowers change with each of the four seasons.
For heart I've a withered tree of Li-ling,
For hair the tangled threads of Sui-yang.[11]
It's not the heat of summer and yet I cringe;
Other than autumn days I still feel sad.
Fishes, one inch, two inches long;
Bamboos, two canes, three canes growing;
Cloud breath darkening over clumps of milfoil,

---

[10] A Taoist adept named Chieh Hsiang, having died at noon at Wu-ch'ang, was
seen at evening in Chien-yeh (Nanking) far away. A shrine was built in his honor,
where white cranes often came to roost. Yü Hsin hints that, though he too
longs to go to Chien-yeh, the capital of the southern court, he lacks Chieh
Hsiang's magical powers. The second line refers to the tale of an old man who
used tortoises to support the legs of his couch. When he died some twenty
years later, the tortoises were found to be still alive. Cranes and tortoises are
stock symbols of longevity.

[11] Li-ling is famous for its camphor trees, many of them old and withered.
Sui-yang is where the philosopher Mo Tzu saw strands of white undyed silk and
sighed to think that they could be made to take on any color the dyer chose.

Essence of gold cherished in the autumn chrysanthemum;
Jujubes sour, pears acid to the bite,
Peaches, garden-grown and wild ones; damsons big and small:
Their fallen leaves half bury my chair,
Their rioting petals fill the room—
Call this the home of a country fellow,
Name it the valley of an ignorant sir.
  I've tried lying down in these shady groves;
So long I'd envied those who had doffed official hatpins.
I have a gate but it's always closed;
No ocean here, yet I've sunk out of sight!
Late spring I shoulder my hoe along with friends;
Fifth month I put on leather coat, ready for chores.[12]
I look into Ko Hung's writings on the properties of medicines,
Pay a visit to Ching Fang's forest of divinations.[13]
Yet these grasses fail to "banish sorrow" from my mind,
These flowers bring no "lasting joy" to the heart.[14]
What use would a bird have being offered wine?
What heart would a fish have to listen to a lute?
  On top of this
The cold and heat here are of a different kind;
They offend my southern nature.
Ts'ui Yin through lack of joy shortened his life;
Wu Chih by constant grieving made himself sick.[15]
House spirits I've stilled by burying stones;
To ward off mountain goblins I've a mirror to flash;[16]

---

[12] The leather protects the shoulders when carrying firewood and other loads.

[13] Ko Hung (4th cen.) is the author of the *Pao-p'u Tzu*, a work on Taoist alchemy. Ching Fang (77–37 B.C.) was an expert on the *I Ching* and author of a work entitled "Collected Forest of the Chou Yi."

[14] "Banish sorrow" and "lasting joy" are names of a kind of plant and flower respectively.

[15] Ts'ui Yin of the Eastern Han died of grief when his superior, General Tou Hsien, refused to heed his admonitions. Wu Chih, friend of Ts'ao P'ei (Emperor Wen of the Wei) and the poets of the Chien-an period, grieved especially that so many of his companions had died in the plague epidemic of A.D. 217.

[16] Stones buried at the four corners of the house protect it from ghosts; goblins flee from a mirror because they are incapable of casting a reflection.

Yet often I'm moved to Chuang Hsieh's kind of singing,
To commit acts as senseless as the order to Wei K'o.[17]
Dusk falling on quiet rooms
Finds old and young hand in hand,
Sons as tousle-headed as those of Wang Pa,
My wife, hair in mallet-bun, like the wife of Liang Hung.[18]
Of parched grain we have two bins,
Of cold vegetables, one garden plot full.
Winds wail and buffet, lashing through the trees;
Skies are bleak and threatening, clouds pressing down.
Gathered by the empty barn, sparrows complain;
Chiding the lazy housewife, cicadas shrill.

　　In the past I pretended to play the pipes,
Trusting to hand-me-down fortune, as the *Wen-yen* says.[19]
Our house was praised for its pervasive virtue,
Our family received gifts of books from the ruler.
On occasion I attended His Majesty in the Tower of the Dark
　　　　Warrior;
Sometimes I waited on him in the Place of Phoenixes,
Granted audience in the Great Hall where sacrificial meats are
　　　　received,
Composing *fu* in the officials' lodge like that on Ch'ang-yang
　　　　Palace.[20]

[17] On the singing of the homesick Chuang Hsieh, see p. 53, n. 3. Wei K'o's father, a minister of the state of Chin in Chou times, in the last stages of illness gave an order that his favorite concubine was to be killed and buried with him. Wei K'o, in view of his father's deranged condition, ignored the order.

[18] Wang Pa and Liang Hung were recluses of the Eastern Han.

[19] The first line refers to the story of a man who pretended to be able to play the pipes and was employed in the orchestra of King Hsüan of Ch'i; the deception was exposed when the king's son and successor forced the members of the orchestra to play one at a time. Yü Hsin is modestly referring to his official service under the Liang. The *Wen-yen* Commentary on the *I Ching* states: "A family that piles up noble deeds is certain to have an abundance of good fortune."

[20] These lines, embodying allusions to various great statesmen and scholars of the Han such as Chia Yi, Yang Hsiung, Cheng Hsüan, and the members of the Pan family, refer to the distinguished history of the Yü family and Yü Hsin's own career as an official.

But then
Mountains crumbled, rivers ran dry;
There was a cracking of ice, a shattering of tiles.
The great bandit worked his usurpation,
The star of our heavens faded for all time.[21]
Things shattered—because free rein was given on Three Peril Hill;
Broke—because there was reckless driving on the Slope of Nine
          Turnings.[22]
Ching K'o had his heartbreak beside the cold waters,
Su Wu his farewell in the autumn wind.[23]
At border mountains, wind and moon filled me with foreboding;
By Lung waters, my liver and bowels broke in two.
The tortoise told me this land was too cold;
Cranes warned of this year's snow.[24]

A man's hundred years—how swift in passing,
Youth's bright flower faded long ago!
I shall not work to wipe out the mishap at Yen-men,
But recall the long flight of the swan across the plains.[25]

[21] These lines refer to the fact that in 548 the military leader Hou Ching revolted against the Liang, seized the capital, and declared himself emperor. Emperor Wu, deposed, died in captivity.

[22] Hou Ching, a northerner, had earlier submitted to Emperor Wu and been enfeoffed and honored by the Liang. Yü Hsin is censuring the lack of caution and forethought evidenced by these actions and the disaster that ensued.

[23] Ching K'o, setting off on an attempt to assassinate the ruler of the enemy state of Ch'in (3d cen. B.C.), took sad farewell of his friends by the cold waters of the Yi River. See p. 98, n. 4. Su Wu, a general of the Han, left China in 100 B.C. to act as envoy to the northern Hsiung-nu tribes and was detained in the north for twenty years. Yü Hsin compares his own departure from the south and detention in the north to the cases of these men.

[24] A ruler of one of the northern dynasties acquired a tortoise which he kept captive for sixteen years until it died. Later the tortoise appeared in a dream to a diviner and complained that it had longed to return to its home in the south but was forced to die a captive in the north. The parallel with Yü Hsin's situation is obvious. When there were heavy snows in the winter of A.D. 281, two white cranes were heard to remark that the snow was as severe as the year when the ancient sage ruler Yao died. Yü Hsin is alluding to the death of Emperor Yüan of the Liang at the hands of northern invaders in the winter of A.D. 554.

[25] The first line alludes to the career of an official of the Former Han who, while governor of Yen-men, was tried for an offense and removed from office. When

I cannot change shape in the Huai or ocean,
I cannot be transmuted like cinnabar or gold.[26]
Having failed to leave my bones to bleach by Dragon Gate,
I end like the horse on the slope, head hung down.[27]
Truly Heaven's workings are dark and devious;
Alas for mankind in the tangle of their maze!

he later resumed office, he was warned by a friend not to try to achieve any outstanding merit in hopes of compensating for his earlier disgrace. The second line refers to the *I Ching*, hexagram #53: "The wild swan slowly crosses the plains, but the traveler does not return." Though Yü Hsin refers to the swan, it is the second part of the statement that weighs upon his mind.

[26] According to Chinese nature lore, sparrows that dive into the ocean are turned into oysters, and pheasants that enter the Huai River become clams. The second line refers to the transformations of Chinese alchemy.

[27] When the mythical sage Yü cut a channel for the Yellow River through the mountains, he created a narrow gorge called Dragon Gate. Fish strong enough to ascend the rapids turned into dragons; those that could not fell back and died. Po Lo, an ancient connoisseur of horses, once encountered a thoroughbred hitched to a wagon of salt and struggling up the slopes of the T'ai-hang Mountains. Yü Hsin is saying that, because he did not die fighting in defense of the Liang, he has now sunk to a position of captivity and disgrace.

EARLY CRITICAL STATEMENTS

ON THE FU FORM

PAN KU (32–92)
PREFACE TO THE "FU ON THE TWO CAPITALS"

The following is the first part of Pan Ku's preface, which takes a laudatory view of the Han period fu, or at least of those works by high government officials that were clearly didactic in intent. (Wen hsüan 1.)

IT HAS BEEN SAID that the *fu* derives from the poetry (*shih*) of ancient times. Long ago, when kings Ch'eng and K'ang passed away, the hymns ceased to sound; when royal beneficence came to an end, poems were no longer composed.[1] When the great Han dynasty first rose to power, each day was taken up with pressing tasks; but by the reigns of emperors Wu and Hsüan (140–49 B.C.) there was at last time to pay due honor to the officials in charge of rites and to give thought to cultural matters. Within the palace were set up the offices of the Metal Horse and the Stone Conduit; outside it were

---

[1] Ch'eng and K'ang were rulers in the golden age of the early Chou (eleventh and tenth centuries B.C.), when most of the hymns and other songs of the *Book of Odes* were said to have been composed.

established the Music Bureau and the post of Harmonizer of Tones.[2] Their purpose was to revive what had fallen into neglect, to restore what had been cut off, thus lending brilliance and color to our glorious dynasty. As a result, the numberless masses rejoiced and were content, and blessings and happy responses appeared in abundance. The songs of the white unicorn, the red goose, the fungus chamber, and the precious caldron were presented at the suburban sacrifices and the ancestral temples, and the auspicious omens of the sacred sparrow, the five phoenixes, the sweet dew, and the yellow dragon were employed in numbering the years.[3] The courtiers who performed literary services, such as Ssu-ma Hsiang-ju, Yü-ch'iu Shou-wang, Tung-fang Shuo, Mei Kao, Wang Pao, and Liu Hsiang, morning and night debated and pondered, daily and monthly presenting their works for consideration. In addition, high officials and great statesmen, such as the imperial secretary Ni K'uan, the master of ritual K'ung Tsang, the palace counselor Tung Chung-shu, the director of the imperial clan Liu Te, the grand tutor to the crown prince Hsiao Wang-chih, and others, from time to time found leisure to compose, some describing conditions on the lower level of society and thereby conveying a reprimand or lesson, some extolling the virtue of those in high places and giving full expression to the ideals of loyalty and filial piety. Mild and well-modulated, full of commendation and praise, such works will shine in generations after, second only to the odes and hymns of antiquity. Therefore, in the reign of Emperor Ch'eng the Filial (32–7 B.C.) they were discussed and recorded, and eventually over a thousand pieces were presented for imperial perusal. From this time on, the culture of our great Han shone with a brilliance matching that of the Three Dynasties of antiquity.

[2] The offices within the palace had surveillance over literary and scholarly activities; the Music Bureau and Harmonizer of Tones were charged with collecting folk songs and composing hymns for state ceremonies.

[3] All these creatures were omens of heavenly favor whose appearance was either celebrated in song or honored in a *nien-hao*, or era name. At this time it became customary for the ruler to declare a new era on the appearance of such an omen and begin the numbering of the years of his reign again. The four era names mentioned here—"sacred sparrow," "five phoenixes," etc.—belong to the end of Emperor Hsüan's reign, the period 61–49 B.C.

PAN KU
SECTION ON FU FROM THE
"TREATISE ON LITERATURE,"

History of the Former Han (Han shu 30).

In this passage, Pan Ku seems to be treating the history of both the fu *and the* shih *forms, and it is not always clear which paragraphs refer to which. Here he takes a much sterner view of the Han* fu, *berating it for its lack of didactic purpose.*

ᛩ

AN OLD TEXT SAYS: That which is not sung but chanted is called a *fu*. He who, ascending to the high places, is able to present a poetic offering (*fu*) is worthy to be a high official.4 In other words, he is moved to composition by his reaction to the things he sees; and, possessing talent and knowledge of great depth and excellence, he is the kind who may be consulted in the conduct of affairs. Therefore he may be ranked among the high officials.

In ancient times, when the feudal lords, ministers, and high officials conducted diplomatic relations with neighboring states, they used subtle words to move one another. Faced with ceremonial occasions of bowing and giving way, they invariably recited selections from the *Odes* in order to convey their ideas. Thus it was possible to distinguish the worthy from the unworthy, and to perceive which states were likely to flourish and which to fade. Therefore Confucius said, "If you do not study the *Odes* you will be unable to speak!"5

After the Spring and Autumn period, the ways of the Chou dynasty gradually fell into disuse. The old diplomatic inquiries with their recitations of songs were no longer carried out among the various states and the men who studied the *Odes* retired from

4 The source of the first statement attributed to the "old text" (*chuan*) is unknown. The second is quoted from the Han period *Mao chuan* or Mao Commentary on the *Book of Odes*, poem #50, where a list of nine types of literary composition which qualify one to be regarded as a high official is given.

5 *Analects* XVI, 13; Confucius addressed the remark to his son.

public life and lived among the common people. It was at this time that the *fu* by men of worth who had failed to realize their ambitions came to be written. The great Confucian scholar Hsün Ch'ing and the minister of Ch'u, Ch'ü Yüan, encountering slander and grieving for their states, both wrote *fu* in order to express their criticisms.[6] All their works are imbued with a spirit of compassion and are in the tradition of the ancient poetry.

Later there appeared Sung Yü and T'ang Le and, after the founding of the Han, Mei Sheng, Ssu-ma Hsiang-ju, and Yang Hsiung. Each strove to outdo the others in ornate and extravagant language, thus obscuring whatever satirical or didactic function his works might have had. This is why Yang Hsiung in time repented that he had written such works, declaring: "The *fu* written by the poets of the *Book of Odes* are both beautiful and well-ordered; the *fu* of the rhetoricians are beautiful but unlicensed. If the disciples of Confucius had been *fu* writers, then we might say that Chia Yi had 'ascended the hall' and Ssu-ma Hsiang-ju had 'entered the inner apartments.' But since they were not, then what is there to be said?"[7]

From the time when Emperor Wu the Filial set up the Music Bureau (*ca.* 120 B.C.) and songs and ballads were collected, we came to have the ditties of Tai and Chao and the airs of Ch'in and Ch'u. All are expressions of sadness and joy which take their inspiration from some particular event. They serve to reveal the manners and customs of the people and to indicate whether their lot is a prosperous or a paltry one.

---

[6] The works attributed to Ch'ü Yüan (*fl. ca.* 300 B.C.) and preserved in the *Ch'u Tz'u* or *Songs of the South* resemble the *fu* in both style and content and are often regarded as part of the same line of literary development. On the *fu* of the philosopher Hsün Ch'ing, see Appendix II, p. 123.

[7] *Fa yen*, sec. 2. The allusion is to *Analects* XI, 14: "Yü has ascended the hall but has not yet entered the inner apartments." In other words, had Confucius approved of works of pure literature such as the Han *fu*, then Chia Yi might be regarded as very promising and Ssu-ma Hsiang-ju as truly accomplished.

TSO SSU (FL. A.D. 300)
PREFACE TO THE "FU ON THE THREE CAPITALS"

Tso Ssu inveighs against poetic license and calls for greater accuracy of fact in the fu. (Wen hsüan 4.)

⚕

THE *Book of Odes* employs six principles, of which the second is called *fu*.[8] Yang Hsiung remarks that "the *fu* written by the poets of the *Book of Odes* are both beautiful and well-ordered."[9] Pan Ku has said, "The *fu* derives from the poetry of ancient times."[10] The rulers of antiquity collected poems in order to observe the nature of the land. Thus, reading of "the green bamboo full and fair," they knew what it was that grew on the banks of the Ch'i in the region of Wei.[11] Reading the line, "He is in the house of planks," they learned what the dwellings of the Western Jung barbarians in the wastes of Ch'in were like.[12] So with complete ease they were able to distinguish the characteristics of each of the eight directions.

But when Ssu-ma Hsiang-ju in his "*Fu* on the Shang-lin Park" speaks of loquats ripening in summer;[13] when Yang Hsiung in his

[8] The six *yi* or principles are six terms that from early times have been used in discussions of the *Book of Odes*. Three of them, *hsing*, *pi*, and *fu*, refer to stylistic devices, the other three, *feng*, *ya*, and *sung*, to the various sections into which the anthology is divided. *Fu* is taken to mean "description," that is, those poems or parts of poems that are mainly concerned with the description of a scene or action. Because the same word came later to be used to designate the rhyme-prose works of the Han, it allowed writers such as Yang Hsiung and Pan Ku to establish what seemed to be a link between the *Book of Odes* and the *fu* form.

[9] *Fa yen* sec. 2.

[10] In the preface to his "*Fu* on the Two Capitals," translated above.

[11] *Odes* #55, "Airs of Wei." An older interpretation would take "green bamboo" as the names of two plants; but for the sake of the parallelism I believe Tso Ssu intended the words to be taken as in the translation.

[12] *Odes* #128, "Airs of Ch'in."

[13] *Lu-chü*, from which the English word loquat derives, is also used at times to designate a type of citrus fruit. See Edward H. Schafer, *The Vermilion Bird: T'ang Images of the South* (Berkeley: University of California Press, 1967), p. 185. It is uncertain which fruit Ssu-ma Hsiang-ju intended.

"*Fu* on the Sweet Springs" presents us with "jade trees in their green luxuriance";[14] when Pan Ku in his "*Fu* on the Western Capital" exclaims over the catching of "paired-eye" fish;[15] or when Chang Heng in his "*Fu* on the Western Metropolis" tells us that Jo, the sea god, was swimming about,[16] we know that they are merely dragging in the names of these rare and outlandish objects in order to enrich and color their works. Instances of this sort of thing are not confined to the examples above. If we look into the matter of fruits and trees, we will know that the ones mentioned in the examples are not native to that region; and if we delve into the question of supernatural beings, we will know that the one cited here would hardly be found in such a locale! As far as words go, it is easy enough to fashion such adornments and fripperies; but from the point of view of meaning they are fictitious and without proof.

If the jade goblet lacks a bottom, no matter how rare it may be, it is useless. If fine words lack a basis in fact, no matter how beautiful they may be, they cannot endure. But although critics unanimously attack the works mentioned above for their lack of care and precision, yet the majority of writers persist in holding them up as models of style. And when an action is repeated, in time it becomes habitual—the outcome is inevitable.

I made up my mind that, using the *fu* on the two capitals as a model, I would compose my own "*Fu* on the Three Capitals." For the mountains and rivers, towns and cities involved, I pored over maps of the area; for the birds, animals, plants, and trees, I checked with local gazetteers; the songs and dances mentioned are in each case those that belong to the folkways of the particular region; the heroes and great men are invariably drawn from the history of its past. Why have I done all this? Because he who puts forth words to make a poem should sing of the appropriate emotion; he who ascends the high places and presents his poetic offering should

---

[14] According to some commentators, these were artificial trees fashioned out of jade. The objection is presumably to the fact that Yang describes them as though they were living, though they may possibly have been a variety of tree not native to the capital.

[15] *Pi-mu*, a type of fish which always swims in pairs, native to the eastern region.

[16] Chang Heng has the sea god swimming in the lake in the palace grounds.

celebrate the sights before him; he who would proclaim the beauty of things must do so by honoring their true nature; and he who would praise actions must do so by sticking to the facts. If there is no truth and no factuality, then how is the reader to believe what he is told?

The importance of exacting tribute on the basis of what is native to each region is made clear in the *Book of Documents*; the need to exercise care in identifying things and placing each in its proper environment is stressed in the *Book of Changes*.[17] I have touched here upon only one aspect of the matter, but the same principles should apply in the ordering of the entire literary work, so that all may be founded upon a sound knowledge of the past.

LIU HSIEH (EARLY 6TH CEN.) "ELUCIDATING THE FU,"

from *The Literary Mind and the Carving of Dragons*
(*Wen-hsin tiao-lung*, sec. 8)

Liu Hsieh's Wen-hsin tiao-lung *is the most detailed and important work of early Chinese literary criticism, treating in its fifty sections both the history of individual literary forms and the broader questions of method, style, and value in literature. In the translation of the section on fu which follows I have been greatly aided by the English translation of the work by Vincent Yu-chung Shih,* The Literary Mind and the Carving of Dragons (*New York: Columbia University Press, 1959*), *and the Japanese translation by Kōzen Hiroshi,* Sekai koten bungaku zenshū XXV (*Tokyo: Chikuma Shobō, 1968*).

THE *Book of Odes* has its six principles, of which the second is called *fu. Fu* means *p'u,* "to set forth;" setting forth colors, unfolding patterns, one gives form to objects and expression to ideas. In ancient times the Duke of Shao called upon the lords and high officials to present their poems and the music masters their

---

[17] References are to the "Tribute of Yü" section of the *Documents* and the explanation of the *wei-chi* hexagram in the *I Ching*.

admonitions and *fu*.[18] An old text says, "He who, ascending to the high places, is able to present a poetic offering (*fu*) is worthy to be a high official." In the Preface to the *Odes*, *fu* is treated the same as the others of the six principles, while in the explanations of the *Kuo yü* and Mao Commentary it is regarded as a different form. If one investigates the gist of these passages, however, they will be seen to refer to a single root and branch. Liu Hsiang clarified the matter by stating that the *fu* was not sung but chanted,[19] and Pan Ku declared it derived from the poetry of ancient times.

When we come to works such as the "Great Tunnel" of Duke Chuang of Cheng or the "Fox Fur" of Shih Wei, we see that they kept the words succinct and the rhymes few, and the compositions are of their own making. But though they accord with the *fu* form, they represent a dim light that has yet to grow brighter.[20] Later, when Ch'ü Yüan composed his *Li sao*, then for the first time the sounds and sights were given full expression. Thus we see that the *fu* received its life from the poets of the *Book of Odes* and was shaped and developed by those of the *Ch'u Tz'u*. With the works on "Ritual" and "Wisdom" by Hsün Ch'ing and "The Wind" and "Fishing" by Sung Yü, it was presented with the title of *fu* or rhyme-prose, marking it off as a territory separate from that of *shih* or poetry. As one among the six principles of the *Odes*, it had been a mere dependent state; now it flourished and grew into a great country. It began its development through the use of the "host-and-guest" form,[21] and then exploited its literary possibilities through an exhaustive treatment of sounds and sights. Thus it

[18] The statement is based on a passage in the *Kuo yü* or "Conversations from the States," *Chou yü*: "The Son of Heaven, when hearing government affairs, had the lords, high officials, and others, down to the gentlemen in their ranks, present their poems, the blind musicians present their lists of precedents, the historiographers present their documents, the music masters their admonitions, those with pupil-less eyes their *fu*," etc.

[19] See p. 113; Liu Hsieh identifies the author of the quotation as Liu Hsiang because Pan Ku adopted most of his material from an earlier work on bibliography by Liu Hsiang.

[20] "Great Tunnel" and "Fox Fur" are brief rhymed works recorded in *Tso chuan*, Yin 1 and Hsi 5 respectively.

[21] I.e., the dialogue form, used by Hsün Ch'ing; see Appendix II, p. 123.

became for the first time a separate form from the *shih* poetry, and under the name of *fu* made its own beginning.

The Ch'in dynasty was not given to literature, though it produced a few works in a mixed *fu* form. The rhetoricians of the early Han followed fashion and wrote new works, Lu Chia the first to pick up the strands, Chia Yi carrying on with the weaving, Mei Sheng and Ssu-ma Hsiang-ju racing with the same wind, Wang Pao and Yang Hsiung galloping with all their might. Mei Kao, Tung-fang Shuo, and others inferior to them turned to the delineation of every conceivable object; a multitude of works accumulated in the reign of Emperor Hsüan (73–49 B.C.), and in the time of Emperor Ch'eng (32–7 B.C.) were examined and collated, a collection of *fu* presented for imperial inspection numbering over a thousand pieces. Thus my inquiry into the origins of the *fu* form has revealed that in fact it came into being in the state of Ch'u and reached its flourishing under the Han.

Works on capitals and palaces, gardens and hunts, or those which described journeys or set forth ideas all helped to "give form to the state and order to the outlying regions," [22] and their purpose is to honor glory and greatness. Having broached the subject in the opening chords of the *hsü* or preface, they brought the last stray ends to conclusion in the final *luan* or reprise, the preface stating the themes and introducing the emotions that underlie the piece, the reprise bringing order to the work as a whole, fulfilling the requirements of the *fu* as a literary form. (It may be noted that the last stanza of the "*No*" was called by its author, Min-ma Fu, a *luan*.[23] So we know that the men of Yin used the *luan* or reprise to bring a harmonious end to their hymns, and the men of Ch'u used it to order their works in the *fu* or rhyme-prose form.) All these compositions fall within the realm of masterful creation and represent the very core and crux of graceful literature.

As for those works that deal with the world of plants, the tribes of birds, the numberless kinds of things in all their profusion of species, the writer encounters a certain object and is moved to

[22] *Chou li*, section on Heaven, "T'ai-tsai."

[23] The poem is #301 in the *Odes*, first of the hymns of Shang or Yin. A passage in *Kuo yü, Lu yü* 2, applies the term *luan* to the end of the hymn.

feeling, observes the way in which it changes and draws a moral. In delineating the form and appearance of the object, he strives for delicacy and conciseness of language; in conveying the symbolic meaning appropriate to each object, he prizes the kind of reasoning that follows naturally from the object itself. These are compositions that belong to the domain of lesser creations, the essence and epitome of skill in the unusual.

Looking into the matter, we find that Hsün Ch'ing put together riddling works, in which the subject often ends by explaining itself; Sung Yü set forth exaggerated tales, the beginning, in fact, of "unlicensed beauty;" Mei Sheng in his poem on the Rabbit Garden conveyed the principals of the scene while adding a touch of newness; Ssu-ma Hsiang-ju in his "Shang-lin Park" used a profusion of species to create an effect of lushness; Chia Yi in his *fu* on the owl applied eloquence to the treatment of emotion and ideas; Wang Pao in his work on the hollow flute exhausted all the variations of sound and sight; Pan Ku's rhyme-prose on the two capitals is clear and refined, correct and well turned out; Chang Heng's rhyme-prose on the two metropolises is fast moving and unusual, copious and rich; Yang Hsiung's work on the palace at Sweet Springs breathes an air of profundity and rareness; Wang Nien-shou's work on the Ling-kuang Palace is imbued with all the energy of movement or flight. These ten writers were all masters of the *fu* style of the Han rhetoricians.

Later we come to Wang Ts'an, admirable and concise, who when he broaches a theme always moves forward with alacrity; Hsü Kan, learned and perceptive, who at times achieved true vigor and brilliance; Tso Ssu and P'an Yüeh, whose achievement lay in the fashioning of large-scale models; Lu Chi and Ch'eng-kung Sui, who made their mark in more popular forms; Kuo P'u, polished and clever, with eloquence and ideas to spare; Yüan Hung, who expressed deep passion, yet managed to neglect neither style nor euphony. These were the chief *fu* writers of the Wei and Chin periods.

Looking into the statement about "ascending the high places," [24] we find that one observes certain objects and is inspired to

[24] The statement in the Mao Commentary, quoted on p. 113, which tells how men of old ascended to high places and, inspired by the scenery about them, recited or composed poems.

feeling. Because the feeling is inspired by a particular object, the ideas of the poem will inevitably be clear and refined. And because the object is observed in terms of the feeling it inspires, the words of the poem will necessarily be well chosen and beautiful. Beautiful words and refined ideas will match and complement each other, like the apportioning of red and purple threads in a piece of woven goods, or the application of black and yellow pigment in a painting. The patterns, though novel, will be supported by sound substance; the colors, though varied, will be laid on a firm base. This is the essential point in fashioning a *fu*.

As for those writers who chase after secondary concerns and display only contemptuous neglect for fundamentals, though they read a thousand *fu*, they will only become more confused about the essentials of the form.[25] They will persevere until they achieve such a profusion of blossoms that it breaks the stem, such plumpness of flesh that it injures the bone. Their works show no respect for earlier models of the form and serve no purpose in encouraging good and censuring evil. This is the reason that Yang Hsiung in later life regretted having indulged in such "carving of insects," that he condemned such works as mere "mist-like gauze."[26]

Tsan:[27]

The *fu* derives from the *shih* poetry form,
A fork in the road, a different line of development;
It describes objects, pictures their appearance,

[25] A reference to the words attributed to Yang Hsiung: "If you read a thousand *fu*, you will be good at writing them." See Introduction, p. 14.

[26] *Fa yen*, sec. 2: "Someone asked me if I was not fond of writing *fu* in my younger days. I replied, 'Yes—as a little boy carves insects or engraves seals. But suddenly one day I said to myself, a grown man does not do such things!' ... Someone asked, 'Is not mist-like gauze the most beautiful of all woven goods?' I replied, 'It is an abuse of the weaving woman's skill!'" Yang Hsiung is comparing the "mist-like gauze," difficult to produce and of little practical use, with the extravagant works in *fu* form of his time.

[27] A passage, usually in rhymed four-character lines, that sums up the principal points in an essay, biography, or other piece of writing.

With a brilliance akin to sculpture or painting.
What is clogged and confined it invariably opens up;
It depicts the commonplace with unbounded charm;
But the goal of the form is beauty well-ordered,
Words retained for their loveliness when weeds have been cut away.

TWO FU OF HSÜN CH'ING

☫

CHAPTER 26 of the *Hsün Tzu*, the collected writings of the Confucian philosopher Hsün Ch'ing or Hsün K'uang (*fl. ca.* 250 B.C.), consists of six poems, designated in the title of the chapter as *fu*. The "Treatise on Literature" in the *Han shu* lists ten works in *fu* form attributed to Hsün Ch'ing, and presumably the six poems in the *Hsün Tzu* represent part of the ten. Because they are thought to be the earliest specimens of works bearing the designation *fu*, they are frequently mentioned in discussions of the evolution of the form, though in scale and content they bear little resemblance to the *fu* attributed to Sung Yü and the early Han writers. As will be seen from the translated examples below, their interest is perhaps more historical than literary. The first five are riddles cast in the form of a dialogue between a minister and another person, usually the sovereign, the solutions to which are "ritual," "wisdom," "clouds," "silk-worm," and "needle" respectively. The last (which may in fact be the fragments of two different poems) identifies itself in its opening lines as a "poem of peril" and is wholly given up to a dolorous description of the kind of moral and political chaos and subversion of values so often bemoaned in the *Li sao* and other poems of the *Ch'u Tz'u*. The poems translated below are the first and fourth of the riddles. They employ a predominantly four-character line.

I

"Now here is a great thing,
Not silk, not cloth,

Yet patterned and striped to form a design;
Not sun, not moon,
Yet spreading light for all the world.
The living through it live out their lives,
The dead are buried by it.
Walled cities because of it are safe,
The three armies because of it are strong.
In pure form it makes a king,
In diluted form, a dictator;
Without a trace of it, one is lost!
I, your servant, am stupid and unknowing—
May I beg Your Majesty to explain it?"
The king replied:
"This thing—is it patterned, yet not colored?
Simple, easy to understand,
Yet embodying the profoundest principles?
Something which the gentleman respects,
But the petty man does not?
Lacking it, does human nature turn into a beast,
But, obtaining it, becomes truly refined?
Does the common man, honoring it, become a sage,
The feudal lord, honoring it, unite the four seas?
Enlightened in the highest, yet quite plain,
Most agreeable in embodiment—
With your permission, I conclude it must be ritual."
Ritual!

II

"There is a thing here,
Naked and bare in form,
From time to time changing shape like a god.
Its benefits cloak the whole world;
It offers adornment to ten thousand generations.
Ritual and music gain completion because of it,
Noble and humble through it can be told apart.
It cares for the old, helps the young to grow—
Only if they have it can they survive.

Yet its name is not lauded;
Instead it is put in the company of the evil.[1]
In performing a service, its body is undone;
In fulfilling its task, its house is destroyed.
Its old ones are cast out,
Though its progeny are gathered in.
The race of man profits from it,
But flying birds do it harm.
I, your servant, an stupid and unknowing—
May I ask the Five Great Ones[2] to divine it for me?"
The Five Great Ones divined and said:
"This thing—is its body fair like that of a girl,
Does it have the head of a horse?
Does it frequently change but not live out its life?
Is it well treated in youth, in old age despised?
Has it father and mother, but knows no male or female?
It slumbers in winter, in summer plays,
Feeding on mulberry, spewing out silk,
Tangled first but later well ordered.
Born in summer, it hates the heat;
Delighting in dampness, it hates the rain.
Chrysalis is its mother,
Moth its father;
Thrice it lies down, thrice rises up,
And then its task is almost done.
This describes the principle of the silkworm."
Silkworm!

[1] To "eat silkworm-fashion" is a common term for greedy and violent encroachment; also the word "silkworm" (*ts'an*) suggests the verb "to oppress" (*ts'an*).

[2] Usually identified by commentators as the Five Emperors, sage rulers of antiquity, when the silkworm was first cultivated, though "Five Great" may be the name of a single person.

SELECTED BIBLIOGRAPHY OF

TRANSLATIONS AND STUDIES

OF THE FU

Birch, Cyril, ed. *Anthology of Chinese Literature, from Early Times to the Fourteenth Century*. New York: Grove Press, 1965.

Bishop, John L., ed. *Studies in Chinese Literature*. Cambridge: Harvard University Press, 1965.

Chen, Shih-hsiang, tr. *Lu Chi, Essay on Literature*. Portland, Me.: Anthoensen Press, 1953. Reprinted in Birch, ed. *Anthology of Chinese Literature*.

Fang, Achilles. "Rhyme-prose on Literature: the *Wen-fu* of Lu Chi," *Harvard Journal of Asiatic Studies*, XIV (1951); reprinted in Bishop, ed., *Studies in Chinese Literature*.

Gaspardone, Émile. "Les deux premiers *fou* de Sseu-ma Siang-jou," *Journal Asiatique*, CCXLVI (no. 4, 1958), 447–52.

Gulik, R. H. van. *Hsi K'ang and his Poetical Essay on the Lute*. Tokyo: Sophia University, 1941.

Hawkes, David. *Ch'u Tz'u: The Songs of the South*. Oxford: Clarendon Press, 1959.

—— "The Quest of the Goddess," *Asia Major*, XIII, (no. 1–2, 1967), 71–94.

Hervouet, Yves. *Un poète de cour sous les Han: Sseu-ma Siang-jou*. Paris: Presses Universitaires de France, 1964.

Hightower, James R. *Topics in Chinese Literature*. Cambridge: Harvard University Press, 1950; rev. ed., 1953. Contains valuable information on older translations of *fu*.

—— "The *Fu* of T'ao Ch'ien," *Harvard Journal of Asiatic Studies*, XVII (1954); reprinted in Bishop, ed., *Studies in Chinese Literature*.

Hightower, James R. "Some Characteristics of Parallel Prose," in *Studia Serica Bernhard Karlgren Dedicata*, 1959; reprinted in Bishop, ed., *Studies in Chinese Literature*.

—— "Chia Yi's 'Owl Fu'," *Asia Major*, VII (no. 1–2, 1959); reprinted in Birch, ed., *Anthology of Chinese Literature*.

Hughes, E. R. *The Art of Letters: Lu Chi's "Wen Fu," A.D. 302*. New York: Pantheon Books (Bollingen Series XXIX), 1951.

—— *Two Chinese Poets: Vignettes of Han Life and Thought*. Princeton: Princeton University Press, 1960. On the *fu* on the Han capitals by Pan Ku and Chang Heng.

Knechtges, David R. "Two Studies on the Han *Fu*," *Parerga*, 1, Seattle: University of Washington, Far Eastern and Russian Institute, 1968.

Le Gros Clark, C. D. *The Prose Poetry of Su Tung P'o*. Shanghai: Kelly and Walsh, 1935.

Margouliès, George. *Le "fou" dans le Wen-siuan*. Paris: P. Geuthner, 1926.

Mather, Richard B. "The Mystical Ascent of the T'ient'ai Mountains: Sun Ch'o's *Yu-T'ien-t'ai-shan Fu*," *Monumenta Serica*, XX (1961), 226–45.

Swann, Nancy Lee, tr. "Journey to the East" (*Tung cheng fu*), by Pan Chao; in her *Pan Chao: Foremost Woman Scholar of China*. New York: The Century Co., 1932.

Waley, Arthur. *170 Chinese Poems*. New York: A. A. Knopf, 1919.

—— *The Temple and Other Poems*. New York: A. A. Knopf, 1923.

—— *Chinese Poems*. London: Allen and Unwin, 1946. Reproduces many of the *fu* translations from the earlier volumes.

Watson, Burton, *Records of the Grand Historian of China, Translated from the Shih chi of Ssu-ma Ch'ien*. 2 vols. New York: Columbia University Press, 1961.

—— *Early Chinese Literature*. New York: Columbia University Press, 1962.

Whitaker, K. P. K. "Tsaur Jyr's Luoshern Fuh" (Ts'ao Chih's *Fu* on the Goddess of the Lo), *Asia Major*, IV (no. 1, 1954), 36–56.

Wilhelm, Hellmut. "The Scholar's Frustration: Notes on a Type of *Fu*," in J. K. Fairbank, ed., *Chinese Thought and Institutions*. Chicago: University of Chicago, 1957.

Zach, Erwin von. *Die chinesische Anthologie*. 2 vols. Cambridge: Harvard University Press, 1958. Translations of the *fu* in the *Wen hsüan*.